INDUSTRIAL SOCIETY AND ITS FUTURE
and Other Works

Other Books By Theodore John Kaczynski

Technological Slavery

Anti-Tech Revolution: Why and How

INDUSTRIAL SOCIETY AND ITS FUTURE
and Other Works

Theodore John Kaczynski

WILDERNESS FRONT

PUBLISHER'S NOTE

The version of *Industrial Society and Its Future* (ISAIF) contained in this volume is the updated version that Theodore John Kaczynski later wrote and had published in the Fitch & Madison editions of his first book: *Technological Slavery, Volume One*. This updated version expands on the notes to the original 1995 manifesto, which was itself republished in the first and second editions of *Technological Slavery*. Regarding the nature of this updated version, Kaczynski wrote, "Though I've made some minor changes for stylistic reasons or for clarity, I have not tried to rewrite ISAIF to bring it up to date. Corrections and major clarifications have been relegated to the notes, the number of which has been increased from 36 to 63."

In addition to *Industrial Society and Its Future,* this slim volume of materials contains various writings that Kaczynski explicitly wanted to be published separately from *Technological Slavery,* preferably by a reliable and true anti-tech organization.

Two further items should be clarified: (1) Kaczynski writes to one individual who is not a public figure. Therefore, their full name has been abbreviated by their initials for the purposes of this publication, and (2) "AJODA" is used as an abbreviation for the magazine *Anarchy: A Journal of Desire Armed.*

Wilderness Front
April 2024

Notice: The quote from Kaczynski above is from his book, *Technological Slavery,* Volume One, Fitch & Madison Publishers, Scottsdale, Arizona, 2022, p. 12.

CONTENTS

PREFACE TO *INDUSTRIAL SOCIETY AND ITS FUTURE* (ISAIF)

ISAIF (*Industrial Society and Its Future*) was first published in 1995 by the *Washington Post*. Unfortunately, the *Washington Post's* version was carelessly transcribed and apparently was never proofread. Consequently, what came out in print was riddled with errors, including the omission of parts of sentences and even of whole sentences. Within the next few months several other versions of ISAIF were published in print or on the Internet, but all were based primarily on the *Washington Post's* version, and the publishers transcribed the *Washington Post's* version as carelessly as the *Washington Post* had transcribed the original, so that further errors were added to those of the *Washington Post*. Every time ISAIF was transcribed more errors were added, and the result was that ISAIF was widely distributed in severely mutilated form, while the original remained publicly unavailable. In 2008, at last, an almost correct version of ISAIF appeared in a collection of my writings titled *The Road to Revolution*, which was brought out by the Swiss publisher Xenia; and then in 2010 Feral House, in the United States, published under the title *Technological Slavery* an improved version of *The Road to Revolution* that included the first truly correct version of ISAIF to become publicly available. It is this version that appears here.

In ISAIF I certainly did not foresee everything; since 1995 I've had to modify my views in several ways. But in general terms this little book has stood the test of time. I often get letters from people who tell me that it is now more relevant than ever, and perhaps many readers will agree. Still, it will be worthwhile to point out here some of the most important ways in which ISAIF went astray.

First, in Paragraphs 163, 171–77 I speculated about the future of the technological society. I no longer think these speculations have any value; they have been superseded by Chapter Two of my book *Anti-Tech Revolution: Why and How*.

Second, in Paragraphs 4, 167 and Notes 31, 32, I allowed for the possibility that the technological society might be eliminated through a gradual process of breakdown and disintegration. But I now think such a course of events is so improbable that it need not be taken into consideration. The technological society may undergo a gradual process of deterioration, but only until a point is reached at which the vital systems that keep the society functioning break down all at once; just as a human body may decline through a long illness until it reaches a point at which its vital systems close down all at the same time, so that it dies.

Third, in Paragraph 154 and Note 29 I considered the possibility that advanced techniques could some day be used to identify children who might become criminals, and to suppress their criminal tendencies through a combination of psychological and biological treatments. This may actually be done in a limited number of individual cases, but I no longer think it is likely to occur on a mass basis. It now seems clear that techniques for controlling human behavior will be excessively difficult to apply on a large scale, if those techniques require individualized decision-making by the people who apply them. Much more effective are techniques that can be applied to the population in general and without distinguishing between individuals, such as the techniques of propaganda. If individualized control of behavior ever occurs on a large scale, it will probably be carried out through sophisticated computer programs that respond to individual differences without any need for individualized decision-making by human beings.

Fourth, in Paragraph 139 I wrote, "It is conceivable that our environmental problems... may some day be settled through a rational, comprehensive plan... ." This may be done with some particular environmental problems, as has actually happened in the case of ozone depletion. But I no longer think there is any chance whatever that *all* of our most important environmental problems will some day be settled on a worldwide basis through a rational, comprehensive plan. See Chapter Two of *Anti-Tech Revolution*.

Ted Kaczynski
February 2021

INDUSTRIAL SOCIETY AND ITS FUTURE (ISAIF)

Introduction

1. The Industrial Revolution and its consequences have been a disaster for the human race. They have greatly increased the life expectancy of those of us who live in "advanced" countries, but they have destabilized society, have made life unfulfilling, have subjected human beings to indignities, have led to widespread psychological suffering (in the Third World to physical suffering as well) and have inflicted severe damage on the natural world. The continued development of technology will worsen the situation. It will certainly subject human beings to greater indignities and inflict greater damage on the natural world, it will probably lead to greater social disruption and psychological suffering,[1] and it may lead to increased physical suffering even in "advanced" countries.

2. The industrial-technological system may survive or it may break down. If it survives, it *may* eventually achieve a low level of physical and psychological suffering, but only after passing through a long and very painful period of adjustment and only at the cost of permanently reducing human beings and many other living organisms to engineered products and mere cogs in the social machine. Furthermore, if the system survives, the consequences will be inevitable: There is no way of reforming or modifying the system so as to prevent it from depriving people of dignity and autonomy.

3. If the system breaks down the consequences will still be very painful. But the bigger the system grows the more disastrous the results of its breakdown will be, so if it is to break down it had best break down sooner rather than later.

4. We therefore advocate a revolution against the industrial system. This revolution may or may not make use of violence; it may be sudden or it may be a relatively gradual process spanning a few decades. We can't predict any of that. But we do outline in a very general way the measures that those who hate the industrial system should take in order to prepare the way for a revolution against that form of society. This is not to be a *political* revolution. Its object will be to overthrow not governments but the economic and technological basis of the present society.

5. In this article we give attention to only some of the negative developments that have grown out of the industrial-technological system. Oth-

er such developments we mention only briefly or ignore altogether. This does not mean that we regard these other developments as unimportant. For practical reasons we have to confine our discussion to areas that have received insufficient public attention or in which we have something new to say. For example, since there are well-developed environmental and wilderness movements, we have written very little about environmental degradation or the destruction of wild nature, even though we consider these to be highly important.

The Psychology of Modern Leftism

6. Almost everyone will agree that we live in a deeply troubled society. One of the most widespread manifestations of the craziness of our world is leftism, so a discussion of the psychology of leftism can serve as an introduction to the discussion of the problems of modern society in general.

7. But what is leftism? During the first half of the 20th century leftism could practically have been identified with socialism. Today the movement is fragmented and it is not clear who can properly be called a leftist. When we speak of leftists in this article we have in mind mainly socialists, collectivists, "politically correct" types, feminists, gay and disability activists, animal-rights activists and the like. But not everyone who is associated with one of these movements is a leftist. What we are trying to get at in discussing leftism is not so much a movement or an ideology as a psychological type, or rather a collection of related types. Thus, what we mean by "leftism" will emerge more clearly in the course of our discussion of leftist psychology. (Also, see paragraphs 227–230.)

8. Even so, our conception of leftism will remain a good deal less clear than we would wish, but there doesn't seem to be any remedy for this. All we are trying to do here is indicate in a rough and approximate way the two psychological tendencies that we believe are the main driving force of modern leftism. We by no means claim to be telling the *whole* truth about leftist psychology. Also, our discussion is meant to apply to modern leftism only. We leave open the question of the extent to which our discussion could be applied to the leftists of the 19th and early 20th centuries.

9. The two psychological tendencies that underlie modern leftism we call *feelings of inferiority* and *oversocialization*. Feelings of inferiority are characteristic of modern leftism as a whole, while oversocialization is

characteristic only of a certain segment of modern leftism; but this segment is highly influential.

Feelings of Inferiority

10. By "feelings of inferiority" we mean not only inferiority feelings in the strict sense but a whole spectrum of related traits: low self-esteem, feelings of powerlessness, depressive tendencies, defeatism, guilt, self-hatred, etc. We argue that modern leftists tend to have some such feelings (possibly more or less repressed), and that these feelings are decisive in determining the direction of modern leftism.

11. When someone interprets as derogatory almost anything that is said about him (or about groups with whom he identifies), we conclude that he has inferiority feelings or low self-esteem. This tendency is pronounced among minority-rights activists, whether or not they belong to the minority groups whose rights they defend. They are hypersensitive about the words used to designate minorities and about anything that is said concerning minorities. The terms "Negro," "oriental," "handicapped," or "chick" for an African, an Asian, a disabled person, or a woman originaly had no derogatory connotation. "Broad" and "chick" were merely the feminine equivalents of "guy," "dude," or "fellow." The negative connotations have been attached to these terms by the activists themselves. Some animal-rights activists have gone so far as to reject the word "pet" and insist on its replacement by "animal companion." Leftish anthropologists go to great lengths to avoid saying anything about primitive peoples that could conceivably be interpreted as negative. They want to replace the word "primitive" with "nonliterate." They seem almost paranoid about anything that might suggest that any primitive culture is inferior to our own. (We do not mean to imply that primitive cultures *are* inferior to ours. We merely point out the hypersensitivity of leftish anthropologists.)

12. Those who are most sensitive about "politically incorrect" terminology are not the average black ghetto-dweller, Asian immigrant, abused woman or disabled person, but a minority of activists, many of whom do not even belong to any "oppressed" group but come from privileged strata of society. Political correctness has its stronghold among university professors, who have secure employment with comfortable salaries, and the majority of whom are heterosexual white males from middle to upper-class families.

13. Many leftists have an intense identification with the problems of groups that have an image of being weak (women), defeated (American Indians), repellent (homosexuals), or otherwise inferior. The leftists themselves feel that these groups are inferior. They would never admit to themselves that they have such feelings, but it is precisely because they do see these groups as inferior that they identify with their problems. (We do not mean to suggest that women, Indians, etc., *are* inferior; we are only making a point about leftist psychology.)

14. Feminists are desperately anxious to prove that women are as strong and as capable as men. Clearly they are nagged by a fear that women may *not* be as strong and as capable as men.

15. Leftists tend to hate anything that has an image of being strong, good and successful. They hate America, they hate Western civilization, they hate white males, they hate rationality. The reasons that leftists give for hating the West, etc., clearly do not correspond with their real motives. They *say* they hate the West because it is warlike, imperialistic, sexist, ethnocentric and so forth, but where these same faults appear in socialist countries or in primitive cultures, the leftist finds excuses for them, or at best he *grudgingly* admits that they exist; whereas he *enthusiastically* points out (and often greatly exaggerates) these faults where they appear in Western civilization. Thus it is clear that these faults are not the leftist's real motive for hating America and the West. He hates America and the West because they are strong and successful.

16. Words like "self-confidence," "self-reliance," "initiative," "enterprise," "optimism," etc., play little role in the liberal and leftist vocabulary. The leftist is anti-individualistic, pro-collectivist. He wants society to solve everyone's problems for them, satisfy everyone's needs for them, take care of them. He is not the sort of person who has an inner sense of confidence in his ability to solve his own problems and satisfy his own needs. The leftist is antagonistic to the concept of competition because, deep inside, he feels like a loser.

17. Art forms that appeal to modern leftish intellectuals tend to focus on sordidness, defeat and despair, or else they take an orgiastic tone, throwing off rational control as if there were no hope of accomplishing anything through rational calculation and all that were left were to immerse oneself in the sensations of the moment.

18. Modern leftish philosophers tend to dismiss reason, science, ob-

jective reality and to insist that everything is culturally relative. It is true that one can ask serious questions about the foundations of scientific knowledge and about how, if at all, the concept of objective reality can be defined. But it is obvious that modern leftish philosophers are not simply cool-headed logicians systematically analyzing the foundations of knowledge. They are deeply involved emotionally in their attack on truth and reality. They attack these concepts because of their own psychological needs. For one thing, their attack is an outlet for hostility, and, to the extent that it is successful, it satisfies the drive for power. More importantly, the leftist hates science and rationality because they classify certain beliefs as true (i.e., successful, superior) and other beliefs as false (i.e., failed, inferior). The leftist's feelings of inferiority run so deep that he cannot tolerate any classification of some things as successful or superior and other things as failed or inferior. This also underlies the rejection by many leftists of the concept of mental illness and of the utility of IQ tests. Leftists are antagonistic to genetic explanations of human abilities or behavior because such explanations tend to make some persons appear superior or inferior to others. Leftists prefer to give society the credit or blame for an individual's ability or lack of it. Thus if a person is "inferior" it is not his fault, but society's, because he has not been brought up properly.

19. The leftist is not typically the kind of person whose feelings of inferiority make him a braggart, an egotist, a bully, a self-promoter, a ruthless competitor. This kind of person has not wholly lost faith in himself. He has a deficit in his sense of power and self-worth, but he can still conceive of himself as having the capacity to be strong, and his efforts to make himself strong produce his unpleasant behavior.[2] But the leftist is too far gone for that. His feelings of inferiority are so ingrained that he cannot conceive of himself as individually strong and valuable. Hence the collectivism of the leftist. He can feel strong only as a member of a large organization or a mass movement with which he identifies himself.

20. Notice the masochistic tendency of leftist tactics. Leftists protest by lying down in front of vehicles, they intentionally provoke police or racists to abuse them, etc. These tactics may often be effective, but many leftists use them not as a means to an end but because they *prefer* masochistic tactics. Self-hatred is a leftist trait.

21. Leftists may claim that their activism is motivated by compassion or by moral principles, and moral principle does play a role for the

leftist of the oversocialized type. But compassion and moral principle cannot be the main motives for leftist activism. Hostility is too prominent a component of leftist behavior; so is the drive for power. Moreover, much leftist behavior is not rationally calculated to be of benefit to the people whom the leftists claim to be trying to help. For example, if one believes that affirmative action is good for black people, does it make sense to demand affirmative action in hostile or dogmatic terms? Obviously it would be more productive to take a diplomatic and conciliatory approach that would make at least verbal and symbolic concessions to white people who think that affirmative action discriminates against them. But leftist activists do not take such an approach because it would not satisfy their emotional needs. Helping black people is not their real goal. Instead, race problems serve as an excuse for them to express their own hostility and frustrated need for power. In doing so they actually harm black people, because the activists' hostile attitude toward the white majority tends to intensify race hatred.

22. If our society had no social problems at all, the leftists would have to *invent* problems in order to provide themselves with an excuse for making a fuss.

23. We emphasize that the foregoing does not pretend to be an accurate description of everyone who might be considered a leftist. It is only a rough indication of a general tendency of leftism.

Oversocialization

24. Psychologists use the term "socialization" to designate the process by which children are trained to think and act as society demands. A person is said to be well socialized if he believes in and obeys the moral code of his society and fits in well as a functioning part of that society. It may seem senseless to say that many leftists are oversocialized, since the leftist is perceived as a rebel. Nevertheless, the position can be defended. Many leftists are not such rebels as they seem.

25. The moral code of our society is so demanding that no one can think, feel and act in a completely moral way. For example, we are not supposed to hate anyone, yet almost everyone hates somebody at some time or other, whether he admits it to himself or not. Some people are so highly socialized that the attempt to think, feel and act morally imposes a severe burden on them. In order to avoid feelings of guilt, they continually have

to deceive themselves about their own motives and find moral explanations for feelings and actions that in reality have a non-moral origin. We use the term "oversocialized" to describe such people.[3]

26. Oversocialization can lead to low self-esteem, a sense of powerlessness, defeatism, guilt, etc. One of the most important means by which our society socializes children is by making them feel ashamed of behavior or speech that is contrary to society's expectations. If this is overdone, or if a particular child is especially susceptible to such feelings, he ends by feeling ashamed of *himself*. Moreover, the thought and the behavior of the oversocialized person are more restricted by society's expectations than are those of the lightly-socialized person. The majority of people engage in a significant amount of naughty behavior. They lie, they commit petty thefts, they break traffic laws, they goof off at work, they hate someone, they say spiteful things or they use some underhanded trick to get ahead of the other guy. The oversocialized person cannot do these things, or if he does do them he generates in himself a sense of shame and self-hatred. The oversocialized person cannot even experience, without guilt, thoughts or feelings that are contrary to the accepted morality; he cannot think "unclean" thoughts. And socialization is not just a matter of morality; we are socialized to conform to many norms of behavior that do not fall under the heading of morality. Thus the oversocialized person is kept on a psychological leash and spends his life running on rails that society has laid down for him. In many oversocialized people this results in a sense of constraint and powerlessness that can be a severe hardship. We suggest that oversocialization is among the more serious cruelties that human beings inflict on one another.

27. We argue that a very important and influential segment of the modern left is oversocialized and that their oversocialization is of great importance in determining the direction of modern leftism. Leftists of the oversocialized type tend to be intellectuals or members of the upper middle class. Notice that university intellectuals[4] constitute the most highly socialized segment of our society and also the most left-wing segment.

28. The leftist of the oversocialized type tries to get off his psychological leash and assert his autonomy by rebelling. But usually he is not strong enough to rebel against the most basic values of society. Generally speaking, the goals of today's leftists are *not* in conflict with the accepted morality. On the contrary, the left takes an accepted moral principle, adopts it as its own, and then accuses mainstream society of violating that principle. Examples:

racial equality, equality of the sexes, helping poor people, peace as opposed to war, nonviolence generally, freedom of expression, kindness to animals. More fundamentally, the duty of the individual to serve society and the duty of society to take care of the individual. All these have been deeply rooted values of our society (or at least of its middle and upper classes[5]) for a long time. These values are explicitly or implicitly expressed or presupposed in most of the material presented to us by the mainstream communications media and the educational system. Leftists, especially those of the oversocialized type, usually do not rebel against these principles but justify their hostility to society by claiming (with some degree of truth) that society is not living up to these principles.

29. Here is an illustration of the way in which the oversocialized leftist shows his real attachment to the conventional attitudes of our society while pretending to be in rebellion against it. Many leftists push for affirmative action, for moving black people into high-prestige jobs, for improved education in black schools and more money for such schools; the way of life of the black "underclass" they regard as a social disgrace. They want to integrate the black man into the system, make him a business executive, a lawyer, a scientist just like upper-middle-class white people. The leftists will reply that the last thing they want is to make the black man into a copy of the white man; instead, they want to preserve African-American culture. But in what does this preservation of African-American culture consist? It can hardly consist in anything more than eating black-style food, listening to black-style music, wearing black-style clothing and going to a black-style church or mosque. In other words, it can express itself only in superficial matters. In all *essential* respects, most leftists of the oversocialized type want to make the black man conform to white middle-class ideals. They want to make him study technical subjects, become an executive or a scientist, spend his life climbing the status ladder to prove that black people are as good as white. They want to make black fathers "responsible," they want black gangs to become nonviolent, etc. But these are exactly the values of the industrial-technological system. The system couldn't care less what kind of music a man listens to, what kind of clothes he wears or what religion he believes in as long as he studies in school, holds a respectable job, climbs the status ladder, is a "responsible" parent, is nonviolent and so forth. In effect, however much he may deny it, the oversocialized leftist wants to integrate the black man into the system and make him adopt its values.

30. We certainly do not claim that leftists, even of the oversocialized type, *never* rebel against the fundamental values of our society. Clearly they sometimes do. Some oversocialized leftists have gone so far as to rebel against one of modern society's most important principles by engaging in physical violence. By their own account, violence is for them a form of "liberation." In other words, by committing violence they break through the psychological restraints that have been trained into them. Because they are oversocialized these restraints have been more confining for them than for others; hence their need to break free of them. But they usually justify their rebellion in terms of mainstream values. If they engage in violence they claim to be fighting against racism or the like.

31. We realize that many objections could be raised to the foregoing thumbnail sketch of leftist psychology. The real situation is complex, and anything like a complete description of it would take several volumes even if the necessary data were available. We claim only to have indicated very roughly the two most important tendencies in the psychology of modern leftism.

32. The problems of the leftist are indicative of the problems of our society as a whole. Low self-esteem, depressive tendencies and defeatism are not restricted to the left. Though they are especially noticeable in the left, they are widespread in our society. And today's society tries to socialize us to a greater extent than any previous society. We are even told by experts how to eat, how to exercise, how to make love, how to raise our kids and so forth.

The Power Process [6]

33. Human beings have a need (probably based in biology) for something that we will call the *power process*. This is closely related to the need for power (which is widely recognized) but it is not quite the same thing. The power process has four elements. The three most clear-cut of these we call goal, effort and attainment of goal. (Everyone needs to have goals whose attainment requires effort, and needs to succeed in attaining at least some of his goals.) The fourth element is more difficult to define and may not be necessary for everyone. We call it autonomy and will discuss it later (paragraphs 42–44).

34. Consider the hypothetical case of a man who can have anything he wants just by wishing for it. Such a man has power, but he will devel-

op serious psychological problems. At first he will have a lot of fun, but by and by he will become acutely bored and demoralized. Eventually he may become clinically depressed. History shows that leisured aristocracies tend to become decadent. This is not true of fighting aristocracies that have to struggle to maintain their power. But leisured, secure aristocracies that have no need to exert themselves usually become bored, hedonistic and demoralized, even though they have power. This shows that power is not enough. One must have goals toward which to exercise one's power.

35. Everyone has goals; if nothing else, to obtain the physical necessities of life: food, water and whatever clothing and shelter are made necessary by the climate. But the leisured aristocrat obtains these things without effort. Hence his boredom and demoralization.

36. Non-attainment of important goals results in death if the goals are physical necessities, and in frustration if non-attainment of the goals is compatible with survival. Consistent failure to attain goals throughout life results in defeatism, low self-esteem or depression.

37. Thus, in order to avoid serious psychological problems, a human being needs goals whose attainment requires effort, and he must have a reasonable rate of success in attaining his goals.

Surrogate Activities

38. But not every leisured aristocrat becomes bored and demoralized. For example, the emperor Hirohito, instead of sinking into decadent hedonism, devoted himself to marine biology, a field in which he became distinguished. When people do not have to exert themselves to satisfy their physical needs they often set up artificial goals for themselves. In many cases they then pursue these goals with the same energy and emotional involvement that they otherwise would have put into the search for physical necessities. Thus the aristocrats of the Roman Empire had their literary pretensions; many European aristocrats a few centuries ago invested tremendous time and energy in hunting, though they certainly didn't need the meat; other aristocracies have competed for status through elaborate displays of wealth; and a few aristocrats, like Hirohito, have turned to science.

39. We use the term "surrogate activity" to designate an activity that is directed toward an artificial goal that people set up for themselves merely in order to have some goal to work toward, or, let us say, merely for

the sake of the "fulfillment" that they get from pursuing the goal. Here is a rule of thumb for the identification of surrogate activities. Given a person who devotes much time and energy to the pursuit of goal X, ask yourself this: If he had to devote most of his time and energy to satisfying his biological needs, and if that effort required him to use his physical and mental faculties in a varied and interesting way, would he feel seriously deprived because he did not attain goal X? If the answer is no, then the person's pursuit of goal X is a surrogate activity. Hirohito's studies in marine biology clearly constituted a surrogate activity, since it is pretty certain that if Hirohito had had to spend his time working at interesting non-scientific tasks in order to obtain the necessities of life, he would not have felt deprived because he didn't know all about the anatomy and life-cycles of marine animals. On the other hand, the pursuit of sex and love (for example) is not a surrogate activity, because most people, even if their existence were otherwise satisfactory, would feel deprived if they passed their lives without ever having a relationship with a member of the opposite sex. (But pursuit of an excessive amount of sex, more than one really needs, can be a surrogate activity.)

40. In modern industrial society only minimal effort is necessary to satisfy one's physical needs. It is enough to go through a training program to acquire some petty technical skill, then come to work on time and exert the very modest effort needed to hold a job. The only requirements are a moderate amount of intelligence and, most of all, simple *obedience*. If one has those, society takes care of one from cradle to grave. (Yes, there is an underclass that cannot take the physical necessities for granted, but we are speaking here of mainstream society.) Thus it is not surprising that modern society is full of surrogate activities. These include scientific work, athletic achievement, humanitarian work, artistic and literary creation, climbing the corporate ladder, acquisition of money and material goods far beyond the point at which they cease to give any additional physical satisfaction, and social activism when it addresses issues that are not important for the activist personally, as in the case of white activists who work for the rights of nonwhite minorities. These are not always *pure* surrogate activities, since for many people they may be motivated in part by needs other than the need to have some goal to pursue. Scientific work may be motivated in part by a drive for prestige, artistic creation by a need to express feelings, militant social activism by hostility. But for most peo-

ple who pursue them, these activities are in large part surrogate activities. For example, the majority of scientists will probably agree that the "fulfillment" they get from their work is more important than the money and prestige they earn.

41. For many if not most people, surrogate activities are less satisfying than the pursuit of real goals (that is, goals that people would want to attain even if their need for the power process were already fulfilled). One indication of this is the fact that, in many or most cases, people who are deeply involved in surrogate activities are never satisfied, never at rest. Thus the money-maker constantly strives for more and more wealth. The scientist no sooner solves one problem than he moves on to the next. The long-distance runner drives himself to run always farther and faster. Many people who pursue surrogate activities will say that they get far more fulfillment from these activities than they do from the "mundane" business of satisfying their biological needs, but that is because in our society the effort required to satisfy the biological needs has been reduced to triviality. More importantly, in our society people do not satisfy their biological needs *autonomously* but by functioning as parts of an immense social machine. In contrast, people generally have a great deal of autonomy in pursuing their surrogate activities.

Autonomy

42. Autonomy as a part of the power process may not be necessary for every individual. But most people need a greater or lesser degree of autonomy in working toward their goals. Their efforts must be undertaken on their own initiative and must be under their own direction and control. Yet most people do not have to exert this initiative, direction and control as single individuals. It is usually enough to act as a member of a *small* group. Thus, if half a dozen people discuss a goal among themselves and make a successful joint effort to attain that goal, their need for the power process will be served. But if they work under rigid orders handed down from above that leave them no room for autonomous decision and initiative, then their need for the power process will not be served. The same is true when decisions are made on a collective basis, if the group making the collective decision is so large that the role of each individual is insignificant.[7]

43. It is true that some individuals seem to have little need for autonomy. Either their drive for power is weak, or they satisfy it by identifying themselves with some powerful organization to which they belong. And then there are unthinking, animal types who seem to be satisfied with a purely physical sense of power (the good combat soldier, who gets his sense of power by developing fighting skills that he is quite content to use in blind obedience to his superiors).

44. But for most people it is through the power process—having a goal, making an *autonomous* effort, and attaining the goal—that self-esteem, self-confidence and a sense of power are acquired. When one does not have adequate opportunity to go through the power process the consequences are (depending on the individual and on the way the power process is disrupted) boredom, demoralization, low self-esteem, inferiority feelings, defeatism, depression, anxiety, guilt, frustration, hostility, spouse or child abuse, insatiable hedonism, abnormal sexual behavior, sleep disorders, eating disorders, etc.[8]

Sources of Social Problems

45. Any of the foregoing symptoms can occur in any society, but in modern industrial society they are present on a massive scale. We aren't the first to mention that the world today seems to be going crazy. This sort of thing is not normal for human societies. There is good reason to believe that primitive man suffered from less stress and frustration and was better satisfied with his way of life than modern man is. It is true that not all was sweetness and light in primitive societies. Abuse of women was common among the Australian aborigines, transsexuality was fairly common among some of the American Indian tribes. But it does appear that *generally speaking* the kinds of problems that we have listed in the preceding paragraph were far less common among primitive peoples than they are in modern society.

46. We attribute the social and psychological problems of modern society to the fact that that society requires people to live under conditions radically different from those under which the human race evolved and to behave in ways that conflict with the patterns of behavior that the human race developed while living under the earlier conditions. It is clear from what we have already written that we consider lack of opportunity to properly experience the power process as the most important of the

abnormal conditions to which modern society subjects people. But it is not the only one. Before dealing with disruption of the power process as a source of social problems we will discuss some of the other sources.

47. Among the abnormal conditions present in modern industrial society are excessive density of population, isolation of man from nature, excessive rapidity of social change and the breakdown of natural small-scale communities such as the extended family, the village or the tribe.

48. It is well known that crowding increases stress and aggression. The degree of crowding that exists today and the isolation of man from nature are consequences of technological progress. All pre-industrial societies were predominantly rural. The Industrial Revolution vastly increased the size of cities and the proportion of the population that lives in them, and modern agricultural technology has made it possible for the Earth to support a far denser population than it ever did before. (Also, technology exacerbates the effects of crowding because it puts increased disruptive powers in people's hands. For example, a variety of noise-making devices: power mowers, radios, motorcycles, etc. If the use of these devices is unrestricted, people who want peace and quiet are frustrated by the noise. If their use is restricted, people who use the devices are frustrated by the regulations. But if these machines had never been invented there would have been no conflict and no frustration generated by them.)

49. For primitive societies the natural world (which usually changes only slowly) provided a stable framework and therefore a sense of security. In the modern world it is human society that dominates nature rather than the other way around, and modern society changes very rapidly owing to technological change. Thus there is no stable framework.

50. The conservatives are fools: They whine about the decay of traditional values, yet they enthusiastically support technological progress and economic growth. Apparently it never occurs to them that you can't make rapid, drastic changes in the technology and the economy of a society without causing rapid changes in all other aspects of the society as well, and that such rapid changes inevitably break down traditional values.

51. The breakdown of traditional values to some extent implies the breakdown of the bonds that hold together traditional small-scale social groups. The disintegration of small-scale social groups is also promoted by the fact that modern conditions often require or tempt individuals to move to new locations, separating themselves from their communities.

Beyond that, a technological society *has to* weaken family ties and local communities if it is to function efficiently. In modern society an individual's loyalty must be first to the system and only secondarily to a small-scale community, because if the internal loyalties of small-scale communities were stronger than loyalty to the system, such communities would pursue their own advantage at the expense of the system.

52. Suppose that a public official or a corporation executive appoints his cousin, his friend or his coreligionist to a position rather than appointing the person best qualified for the job. He has permitted personal loyalty to supersede his loyalty to the system, and that is "nepotism" or "discrimination," both of which are terrible sins in modern society. Would-be industrial societies that have done a poor job of subordinating personal or local loyalties to loyalty to the system are usually very inefficient. (Look at Latin America.) Thus an advanced industrial society can tolerate only those small-scale communities that are emasculated, tamed and made into tools of the system.[9]

53. Crowding, rapid change and the breakdown of communities have been widely recognized as sources of social problems. But we do not believe they are enough to account for the extent of the problems that are seen today.

54. A few pre-industrial cities were very large and crowded, yet their inhabitants do not seem to have suffered from psychological problems to the same extent as modern man. In America today there still are uncrowded rural areas, and we find there the same problems as in urban areas, though the problems tend to be less acute in the rural areas.[10] Thus crowding does not seem to be the decisive factor.

55. On the growing edge of the American frontier during the 19th century, the mobility of the population probably broke down extended families and small-scale social groups to at least the same extent as these are broken down today. In fact, many nuclear families lived by choice in such isolation, having no neighbors within several miles, that they belonged to no community at all,[11] yet they do not seem to have developed problems as a result.

56. Furthermore, change in American frontier society was very rapid and deep. A man might be born and raised in a log cabin, outside the reach of law and order and fed largely on wild meat; and by the time he arrived at old age he might be working at a regular job and living in an

ordered community with effective law enforcement. This was a deeper change than that which typically occurs in the life of a modern individual, yet it does not seem to have led to psychological problems. In fact, 19th-century American society had an optimistic and self-confident tone, quite unlike that of today's society.[12]

57. The difference, we argue, is that modern man has the sense (largely justified) that change is *imposed* on him, whereas the 19th-century frontiersman had the sense (also largely justified) that he created change himself, by his own choice. Thus a pioneer settled on a piece of land of his own choosing and made it into a farm through his own effort. In those days an entire county might have only a couple of hundred inhabitants, and was a far more isolated and autonomous entity than a modern county is. Hence the pioneer farmer participated as a member of a relatively small group in the creation of a new, ordered community. One may well question whether the creation of this community was an improvement, but at any rate it satisfied the pioneer's need for the power process.

58. It would be possible to give other examples of societies in which there has been rapid change and/or lack of close community ties without the kind of massive behavioral aberration that is seen in today's industrial society. We contend that the most important cause of social and psychological problems in modern society is the fact that people have insufficient opportunity to go through the power process in a normal way. We don't mean to say that modern society is the only one in which the power process has been disrupted. Probably most if not all civilized societies have interfered with the power process to a greater or lesser extent. But in modern industrial society the problem has become particularly acute. Leftism, at least in its recent (mid- to late-20th century) form, is in part a symptom of deprivation with respect to the power process.

Disruption of the Power Process in Modern Society

59. We divide human drives into three groups: (1) those drives that can be satisfied with minimal effort; (2) those that can be satisfied but only at the cost of serious effort; (3) those that cannot be adequately satisfied no matter how much effort one makes. The power process is the process of satisfying the drives of the second group. The more drives there are in the third group, the more there is frustration, anger, eventually defeatism, depression, etc.

60. In modern industrial society natural human drives tend to be pushed into the first and third groups, and the second group tends to consist increasingly of artificially created drives.

61. In primitive societies, physical necessities generally fall into group 2: They can be obtained, but only at the cost of serious effort. But modern society tends to guarantee the physical necessities to everyone[13] in exchange for only minimal effort, hence physical needs are pushed into group 1. (There may be disagreement about whether the effort needed to hold a job is "minimal"; but usually, in lower- to middle-level jobs, whatever effort is required is merely that of *obedience*. You sit or stand where you are told to sit or stand and do what you are told to do in the way you are told to do it. Seldom do you have to exert yourself seriously, and in any case you have hardly any autonomy in work, so that the need for the power process is not well served.)

62. Social needs, such as sex, love and status, often remain in group 2 in modern society, depending on the situation of the individual.[14] But, except for people who have a particularly strong drive for status, the effort required to fulfill the social drives is insufficient to satisfy adequately the need for the power process.

63. So certain artificial needs have been created that fall into group 2, hence serve the need for the power process. Advertising and marketing techniques have been developed that make many people feel they need things that their grandparents never desired or even dreamed of. It requires serious effort to earn enough money to satisfy these artificial needs, hence they fall into group 2. (But see paragraphs 80–82.) Modern man must satisfy his need for the power process largely through pursuit of the artificial needs created by the advertising and marketing industry,[15] and through surrogate activities.

64. It seems that for many people, maybe the majority, these artificial forms of the power process are insufficient. A theme that appears repeatedly in the writings of the social critics of the second half of the 20th century is the sense of purposelessness that afflicts many people in modern society. (This purposelessness is often called by other names, such as "anomie" or "middle-class vacuity.") We suggest that the so-called "identity crisis" is actually a search for a sense of purpose, often for commitment to a suitable surrogate activity. It may be that existentialism is in large part a response to the purposelessness of modern life.[16] Very widespread in mod-

ern society is the search for "fulfillment." But we think that for the majority of people an activity whose main goal is fulfillment (that is, a surrogate activity) does not bring completely satisfactory fulfillment. In other words, it does not fully satisfy the need for the power process. (See paragraph 41.) That need can be fully satisfied only through activities that have some external goal, such as physical necessities, sex, love, status, revenge, etc.

65. Moreover, where goals are pursued through earning money, climbing the status ladder or functioning as part of the system in some other way, most people are not in a position to pursue their goals *autonomously*. Most workers are someone else's employee and, as we pointed out in paragraph 61, must spend their days doing what they are told to do in the way they are told to do it. Even most people who are in business for themselves have only limited autonomy. It is a chronic complaint of small-business persons and entrepreneurs that their hands are tied by excessive government regulation. Some of these regulations are doubtless unnecessary, but for the most part government regulations are essential and inevitable parts of our extremely complex society. A large portion of small business today operates on the franchise system. It was reported in the *Wall Street Journal* a few years ago that many of the franchise-granting companies require applicants for franchises to take a personality test that is designed to *exclude* those who have creativity and initiative, because such persons are not sufficiently docile to go along obediently with the franchise system.[17] This excludes from small business many of the people who most need autonomy.

66. Today people live more by virtue of what the system does *for* them or *to* them than by virtue of what they do for themselves. And what they do for themselves is done more and more along channels laid down by the system. Opportunities tend to be those that the system provides, the opportunities must be exploited in accord with rules and regulations,[18] and techniques prescribed by experts must be followed if there is to be a chance of success.

67. Thus the power process is disrupted in our society through a deficiency of real goals and a deficiency of autonomy in the pursuit of goals. But it is also disrupted because of those human drives that fall into group 3: the drives that one cannot adequately satisfy no matter how much effort one makes. One of these drives is the need for security. Our lives depend on decisions made by other people, we have no control over these deci-

sions and usually we do not even know the people who make them. ("We live in a world in which relatively few people—maybe 500 or 1,000—make the important decisions."—Philip B. Heymann of Harvard Law School[19]). Our lives depend on whether safety standards at a nuclear power-plant are properly maintained; on how much pesticide is allowed to get into our food or how much pollution into our air; on how skillful (or incompetent) our doctor is; whether we lose or get a job may depend on decisions made by government economists or corporation executives; and so forth. Most individuals are not in a position to secure themselves against these threats to more than a very limited extent. The individual's search for security is therefore frustrated, which leads to a sense of powerlessness.

68. It may be objected that primitive man is physically less secure than modern man, as is shown by his shorter life-expectancy; hence modern man suffers from less, not more than the amount of insecurity that is normal for human beings. But psychological security does not closely correspond with physical security. What makes us *feel* secure is not so much objective security as a sense of confidence in our ability to take care of ourselves. Primitive man, threatened by a fierce animal or by hunger, can fight in self-defense or travel in search of food. He has no certainty of success in these efforts, but he is by no means helpless against the things that threaten him. The modern individual on the other hand is threatened by many things against which he is helpless: nuclear accidents, carcinogens in food, environmental pollution, war, increasing taxes, invasion of his privacy by large organizations, nationwide social or economic phenomena that may disrupt his way of life.

69. It is true that primitive man is powerless against some of the things that threaten him; disease for example. But he can accept the risk of disease stoically. It is part of the nature of things, it is no one's fault, unless it is the fault of some imaginary, impersonal demon.[20] But threats to the modern individual tend to be *man-made*. They are not the results of chance but are *imposed* on him by other persons whose decisions he, as an individual, is unable to influence. Consequently he feels frustrated, humiliated and angry.

70. Thus primitive man for the most part has his security in his own hands (either as an individual or as a member of a *small* group), whereas the security of modern man is in the hands of persons or organizations that are too remote or too large for him to be able personally to influence

them. So modern man's drive for security tends to fall into groups 1 and 3; in some areas (food, shelter, etc.) his security is assured at the cost of only trivial effort, whereas in other areas he *cannot* attain security. (The foregoing greatly simplifies the real situation, but it does indicate in a rough, general way how the condition of modern man differs from that of primitive man.)

71. People have many transitory drives or impulses that are necessarily frustrated in modern life, hence fall into group 3. One may become angry, but modern society cannot permit fighting. In many situations it does not even permit verbal aggression. When going somewhere one may be in a hurry, or one may be in a mood to travel slowly, but one generally has no choice but to move with the flow of traffic and obey the traffic signals. One may want to do one's work in a different way, but usually one can work only according to the rules laid down by one's employer. In many other ways as well, modern man is strapped down by a network of rules and regulations (explicit or implicit) that frustrate many of his impulses and thus interfere with the power process. Most of these regulations cannot be dispensed with, because they are necessary for the functioning of industrial society.

72. Modern society is in certain respects extremely permissive. In matters that are irrelevant to the functioning of the system we can generally do what we please. We can believe in any religion we like (as long as it does not encourage behavior that is dangerous to the system). We can go to bed with anyone we like (as long as we practice "safe sex"). We can do anything we like as long as it is *unimportant*. But in all *important* matters the system tends increasingly to regulate our behavior.

73. Behavior is regulated not only through explicit rules and not only by the government. Control is often exercised through indirect coercion or through psychological pressure or manipulation, and by organizations other than the government, or by the system as a whole. Most large organizations use some form of propaganda[21] to manipulate public attitudes or behavior. Propaganda is not limited to "commercials" and advertisements, and sometimes it is not even consciously intended as propaganda by the people who make it. For instance, the content of entertainment programming is a powerful form of propaganda. An example of indirect coercion: There is no law that says we have to go to work every day and follow our employer's orders. Legally there is nothing to prevent us from going to

live in the wild like primitive people or from going into business for ourselves. But in practice there is very little wild country left, and there is room in the economy for only a limited number of small-business owners. Hence most of us can survive only as someone else's employee.

74. We suggest that modern man's obsession with longevity, and with maintaining physical vigor and sexual attractiveness to an advanced age, is a symptom of unfulfillment resulting from deprivation with respect to the power process. The "mid-life crisis" also is such a symptom. So is the lack of interest in having children that is fairly common in modern society but almost unheard-of in primitive societies.

75. In primitive societies life is a succession of stages. The needs and purposes of one stage having been fulfilled, there is no particular reluctance about passing on to the next stage. A young man goes through the power process by becoming a hunter, hunting not for sport or for fulfillment but to get meat that is necessary for food. (In young women the process is more complex, with greater emphasis on social power; we won't discuss that here.) This phase having been successfully passed through, the young man has no reluctance about settling down to the responsibilities of raising a family. (In contrast, some modern people indefinitely postpone having children because they are too busy seeking some kind of "fulfillment." We suggest that the fulfillment they need is adequate experience of the power process—with real goals instead of the artificial goals of surrogate activities.) Again, having successfully raised his children, going through the power process by providing them with the physical necessities, the primitive man feels that his work is done and he is prepared to accept old age[22] (if he survives that long) and death. Many modern people, on the other hand, are disturbed by the prospect of physical deterioration and death, as is shown by the amount of effort they expend in trying to maintain their physical condition, appearance and health. We argue that this is due to unfulfillment resulting from the fact that they have never put their physical powers to any practical use, have never gone through the power process using their bodies in a serious way. It is not the primitive man, who has used his body daily for practical purposes, who fears the deterioration of age, but the modern man, who has never had a practical use for his body beyond walking from his car to his house. It is the man whose need for the power process has been satisfied during his life who is best prepared to accept the end of that life.

76. In response to the arguments of this section someone will say, "Society must find a way to give people the opportunity to go through the power process." This won't work for those who need autonomy in the power process. For such people the value of the opportunity is destroyed by the very fact that society gives it to them. What they need is to find or make their own opportunities. As long as the system *gives* them their opportunities it still has them on a leash. To attain autonomy they must get off that leash.

How Some People Adjust

77. Not everyone in industrial-technological society suffers from psychological problems. Some people even profess to be quite satisfied with society as it is. We now discuss some of the reasons why people differ so greatly in their response to modern society.

78. First, there doubtless are innate differences in the strength of the drive for power. Individuals with a weak drive for power may have relatively little need to go through the power process, or at least relatively little need for autonomy in the power process. These are docile types who would have been happy as plantation darkies in the Old South. (We don't mean to sneer at the "plantation darkies" of the Old South. To their credit, most of the slaves were *not* content with their servitude. We do sneer at people who *are* content with servitude.)

79. Some people may have some exceptional drive, in pursuing which they satisfy their need for the power process. For example, those who have an unusually strong drive for social status may spend their whole lives climbing the status ladder without ever getting bored with that game.

80. People vary in their susceptibility to advertising and marketing techniques. Some people are so susceptible that, even if they make a great deal of money, they cannot satisfy their constant craving for the shiny new toys that the marketing industry dangles before their eyes. So they always feel hard-pressed financially even if their income is large, and their cravings are frustrated.

81. Some people have low susceptibility to advertising and marketing techniques. These are the people who aren't interested in money. Material acquisition does not serve their need for the power process.

82. People who have medium susceptibility to advertising and marketing techniques are able to earn enough money to satisfy their craving for goods and services, but only at the cost of serious effort (putting

in overtime, taking a second job, earning promotions, etc.). Thus material acquisition serves their need for the power process. But it does not necessarily follow that their need is fully satisfied. They may have insufficient autonomy in the power process (their work may consist in following orders) and some of their drives may be frustrated (e.g., security, aggression). (We are guilty of oversimplification in paragraphs 80–82 because we have assumed that the desire for material acquisition is entirely a creation of the advertising and marketing industry. Of course, it's not that simple.)

83. Some people partly satisfy their need for power by identifying themselves with a powerful organization or a mass movement. An individual lacking goals or power joins a movement or an organization, adopts its goals as his own, then works toward those goals. When some of the goals are attained, the individual, even though his personal efforts have played only an insignificant part in the attainment of the goals, feels (through his identification with the movement or organization) as if he had gone through the power process. This phenomenon was exploited by the Fascists, Nazis and Communists. Our society uses it too, though less crudely. Example: Manuel Noriega was an irritant to the U.S. (goal: punish Noriega). The U.S. invaded Panama (effort) and punished Noriega (attainment of goal). The U.S. went through the power process and many Americans, because of their identification with the U.S., experienced the power process vicariously. Hence the widespread public approval of the Panama invasion; it gave people a sense of power.[23] We see the same phenomenon in armies, corporations, political parties, humanitarian organizations, religious or ideological movements. In particular, leftist movements tend to attract people who are seeking to satisfy their need for power. But for most people, identification with a large organization or a mass movement does not fully satisfy the need for power.

84. Another way in which people satisfy their need for the power process is through surrogate activities. As we explained in paragraphs 38–40, a surrogate activity is an activity that is directed toward an artificial goal that the individual pursues for the sake of the "fulfillment" that he gets from pursuing the goal, not because he needs to attain the goal itself. For instance, there is no practical motive for building enormous muscles, hitting a little white ball into a hole or acquiring a complete series of postage stamps. Yet many people in our society devote themselves with passion to bodybuilding, golf or stamp-collecting. Some people are more

"other-directed" than others, and therefore will more readily attach importance to a surrogate activity simply because the people around them treat it as important or because society tells them it is important. That is why some people get very serious about essentially trivial activities such as sports, or bridge, or chess, or arcane scholarly pursuits, whereas others who are more clear-sighted never see these things as anything but the surrogate activities that they are, and consequently never attach enough importance to them to satisfy their need for the power process in that way. It only remains to point out that in many cases a person's way of earning a living is also a surrogate activity. Not a *pure* surrogate activity, since part of the motive for the activity is to gain the physical necessities and (for some people) social status and the luxuries that advertising makes them want. But many people put into their work far more effort than is necessary to earn whatever money and status they require, and this extra effort constitutes a surrogate activity. This extra effort, together with the emotional investment that accompanies it, is one of the most potent forces acting toward the continual development and perfecting of the system, with negative consequences for individual freedom. (See paragraph 131.) Especially, for the most creative scientists and engineers, work tends to be largely a surrogate activity. This point is so important that it deserves a separate discussion, which we shall give in a moment (paragraphs 87–92).

85. In this section we have explained how many people in modern society do satisfy their need for the power process to a greater or lesser extent. But we think that for the majority of people the need for the power process is not fully satisfied. In the first place, those who have an insatiable drive for status, or who get firmly "hooked" on a surrogate activity, or who identify strongly enough with a movement or an organization to satisfy their need for power in that way, are exceptional personalities. Others are not fully satisfied with surrogate activities or by identification with an organization. (See paragraphs 41, 64.) In the second place, too much control is imposed by the system through explicit regulation or through socialization, which results in a deficiency of autonomy, and in frustration due to the impossibility of attaining certain goals and the necessity of restraining too many impulses.

86. But even if most people in industrial-technological society were well satisfied, we (FC) would still be opposed to that form of society, because (among other reasons) we consider it demeaning to fulfill one's need

for the power process through surrogate activities or through identification with an organization, rather than through pursuit of real goals.

The Motives of Scientists

87. Science and technology provide the most important examples of surrogate activities. Some scientists claim that they are motivated by "curiosity" or by a desire to "benefit humanity." But it is easy to see that neither of these can be the principal motive of most scientists. As for "curiosity," that notion is simply absurd. Most scientists work on highly specialized problems that are not the object of any normal curiosity. For example, is an astronomer, a mathematician or an entomologist curious about the properties of isopropyltrimethylmethane? Of course not. Only a chemist is curious about such a thing, and he is curious about it only because chemistry is his surrogate activity. Is the chemist curious about the appropriate classification of a new species of beetle? No. That question is of interest only to the entomologist, and he is interested in it only because entomology is his surrogate activity. If the chemist and the entomologist had to exert themselves seriously to obtain the physical necessities, and if that effort exercised their abilities in an interesting way but in some nonscientific pursuit, then they wouldn't give a damn about isopropyltrimethylmethane or the classification of beetles. Suppose that lack of funds for postgraduate education had led the chemist to become an insurance broker instead of a chemist. In that case he would have been very interested in insurance matters but would have cared nothing about isopropyltrimethylmethane. In any case it is not normal to put into the satisfaction of mere curiosity the amount of time and effort that scientists put into their work. The "curiosity" explanation of the scientists' motive just doesn't stand up.

88. The "benefit of humanity" explanation doesn't work any better. Some scientific work has no conceivable relation to the welfare of the human race—most of archaeology or comparative linguistics, for example. Some other areas of science present obviously dangerous possibilities. Yet scientists in these areas are just as enthusiastic about their work as those who develop vaccines or study air pollution. Consider the case of Dr. Edward Teller, who had an obvious emotional involvement in promoting nuclear power-plants. Did this involvement stem from a desire to benefit humanity? If so, then why didn't Dr. Teller get emotional about other "humanitarian" causes? If he was such a humanitarian then why did he help to

develop the hydrogen bomb? As with many other scientific achievements, it is very much open to question whether nuclear power-plants actually do benefit humanity. Does the cheap electricity outweigh the accumulating waste and the risk of accidents? Dr. Teller saw only one side of the question. Clearly his emotional involvement with nuclear power arose not from a desire to "benefit humanity" but from the personal fulfillment he got from his work and from seeing it put to practical use.

89. The same is true of scientists generally. With possible rare exceptions, their motive is neither curiosity nor a desire to benefit humanity but the need to go through the power process: to have a goal (a scientific problem to solve), to make an effort (research) and to attain the goal (solution of the problem). Science is a surrogate activity because scientists work mainly for the fulfillment they get out of the work itself.

90. Of course, it's not that simple. Other motives do play a role for many scientists. Money and status, for example. Some scientists may be persons of the type who have an insatiable drive for status (see paragraph 79) and this may provide much of the motivation for their work. No doubt the majority of scientists, like the majority of the general population, are more or less susceptible to advertising and marketing techniques and need money to satisfy their craving for goods and services. Thus science is not a *pure* surrogate activity. But it is in large part a surrogate activity.

91. Also, science and technology constitute a powerful mass movement, and many scientists gratify their need for power through identification with this mass movement. (See paragraph 83.)

92. Thus science marches on blindly, without regard to the real welfare of the human race or to any other standard, obedient only to the psychological needs of the scientists and of the government officials and corporation executives who provide the funds for research.[24]

The Nature of Freedom

93. We are going to argue that industrial-technological society cannot be reformed in such a way as to prevent it from progressively narrowing the sphere of human freedom. But because "freedom" is a word that can be interpreted in many ways, we must first make clear what kind of freedom we are concerned with.

94. By "freedom" we mean the opportunity to go through the power process—with real goals, not the artificial goals of surrogate activities—and

without interference, manipulation or supervision from anyone, especially from any large organization. Freedom means being in control (either as an individual or as a member of a *small* group) of the life-and-death issues of one's existence: food, clothing, shelter and defense against whatever threats there may be in one's environment. Freedom means having power; not the power to control other people but the power to control the circumstances of one's own life.[25] One does not have freedom if anyone else (especially a large organization) has power over one, no matter how benevolently, tolerantly and permissively that power may be exercised. It is important not to confuse freedom with mere permissiveness. (See paragraph 72.)

95. It is said that we live in a free society because we have a certain number of constitutionally guaranteed rights. But these are not as important as they seem. The degree of personal freedom that exists in a society is determined more by the economic and technological structure of the society than by its laws or its form of government.[26] Most of the Indian nations of New England were monarchies,[27] and many of the cities of the Italian Renaissance were controlled by dictators. But in reading about these societies one gets the impression that they allowed far more personal freedom than our society does. In part this was because they lacked efficient mechanisms for enforcing the ruler's will: There were no modern, well-organized police forces, no rapid long-distance communications, no surveillance cameras, no dossiers of information about the lives of average citizens. Hence it was relatively easy to evade control.

96. As for our constitutional rights, consider for example that of freedom of the press. We certainly don't mean to knock that right; it is a very important tool for limiting concentration of political power and for keeping those who do have political power in line by publicly exposing any misbehavior on their part. But freedom of the press is of very little use to the average citizen as an individual. The mass media are mostly under the control of large organizations that are integrated into the system. Anyone who has a little money can have something printed, or can distribute it on the Internet or in some such way, but what he has to say will be swamped by the vast volume of material put out by the media, hence will have no practical effect. To make an impression on society with words is therefore almost impossible for most individuals and small groups. Take us for example. If we had never done anything violent and had submitted the present writings to a publisher, they probably would not have been

accepted. If they had been accepted and published, they probably would not have attracted many readers, because it's more fun to watch the entertainment put out by the media than to read a sober essay. Even if these writings had had many readers, most of those readers would soon have forgotten what they had read as their minds were flooded by the mass of material to which the media expose them. In order to get our message before the public with some chance of making a lasting impression, we've had to kill people.

97. Constitutional rights are useful up to a point, but they do not serve to guarantee much more than what might be called the bourgeois conception of freedom. According to the bourgeois conception, a "free" man is essentially an element of a social machine and has only a certain set of prescribed and delimited freedoms; freedoms that are designed to serve the needs of the social machine more than those of the individual. Thus the bourgeois's "free" man has economic freedom because that promotes growth and progress; he has freedom of the press because public criticism restrains misbehavior by political leaders; he has a right to a fair trial because imprisonment at the whim of the powerful would be bad for the system. This was clearly the attitude of Simón Bolívar. To him, people deserved liberty only if they used it to promote progress (progress as conceived by the bourgeois).[28] Other bourgeois thinkers have taken a similar view of freedom as a mere means to collective ends. Chester C. Tan explains the philosophy of the Kuomintang leader Hu Han-Min: "An individual is granted rights because he is a member of society and his community life requires such rights. By community Hu meant the whole society or the nation."[29] And Tan states that according to Carsun Chang (Chang Chun-Mai, head of the State Socialist Party in China) freedom had to be used in the interest of the state and of the people as a whole.[30] But what kind of freedom does one have if one can use it only as someone else prescribes? Our conception of freedom is not that of Bolívar, Hu, Chang or other bourgeois theorists. The trouble with such theorists is that they have made the development and application of social theories their surrogate activity. Consequently the theories are designed to serve the needs of the theorists more than the needs of any people who may be unlucky enough to live in a society on which the theories are imposed.

98. One more point to be made in this section: It should not be assumed that a person has enough freedom just because he *says* he has

enough. Freedom is restricted in part by psychological controls of which people are unconscious, and moreover many people's ideas of what constitutes freedom are governed more by social convention than by their real needs. For example, it's likely that many leftists of the oversocialized type would say that most people, including themselves, are socialized too little rather than too much, yet the oversocialized leftist pays a heavy psychological price for his high level of socialization.

Some Principles of History

99. Think of history as the sum of two components: an erratic component that consists of unpredictable events that follow no discernible pattern, and a regular component that consists of long-term historical trends. Here we are concerned with the long-term trends.

100. *First Principle.* If a *small* change is made that affects a long-term historical trend, then the effect of that change will almost always be transitory—the trend will soon revert to its original state. (Example: A reform movement designed to clean up political corruption in a society rarely has more than a short-term effect; sooner or later the reformers relax and corruption creeps back in. The level of political corruption in a given society tends to remain constant, or to change only slowly with the evolution of the society. Normally, a political cleanup will be permanent only if accompanied by widespread social changes; a *small* change in the society won't be enough.) If a small change in a long-term historical trend appears to be permanent, it is only because the change acts in the direction in which the trend is already moving, so that the trend is not altered but only pushed a step ahead.

101. The first principle is almost a tautology. If a trend were not stable with respect to small changes, it would wander at random rather than following a definite direction; in other words, it would not be a long-term trend at all.

102. *Second Principle.* If a change is made that is sufficiently large to alter permanently a long-term historical trend, then it will alter the society as a whole. In other words, a society is a system in which all parts are interrelated, and you can't permanently change any important part without changing all other parts as well.

103. *Third Principle.* If a change is made that is large enough to alter permanently a long-term trend, then the consequences for the society as a

whole cannot be predicted in advance. (Unless various other societies have passed through the same change and have all experienced the same consequences, in which case one can predict on empirical grounds that another society that passes through the same change will be likely to experience similar consequences.)

104. *Fourth Principle.* A new kind of society cannot be designed on paper. That is, you cannot plan out a new form of society in advance, then set it up and expect it to function as it was designed to do.

105. The third and fourth principles result from the complexity of human societies. A change in human behavior will affect the economy of a society and its physical environment; the economy will affect the environment and vice versa, and the changes in the economy and the environment will affect human behavior in complex, unpredictable ways; and so forth. The network of causes and effects is far too complex to be untangled and understood.

106. *Fifth Principle.* People do not consciously and rationally choose the form of their society. Societies develop through processes of social evolution that are not under rational human control.

107. The fifth principle is a consequence of the other four.

108. To illustrate: By the first principle, generally speaking an attempt at social reform either acts in the direction in which the society is developing anyway (so that it merely accelerates a change that would have occurred in any case) or else it has only a transitory effect, so that the society soon slips back into its old groove. To make a lasting change in the direction of development of any important aspect of a society, reform is insufficient and revolution is required. (A revolution does not necessarily involve an armed uprising or the overthrow of a government.) By the second principle, a revolution never changes only one aspect of a society, it changes the whole society; and by the third principle changes occur that were never expected or desired by the revolutionaries. By the fourth principle, when revolutionaries or utopians set up a new kind of society, it never works out as planned.

109. The American Revolution does not provide a counterexample. The American "Revolution" was not a revolution in our sense of the word, but a war of independence followed by a rather far-reaching political reform. The Founding Fathers did not change the direction of development of American society, nor did they aspire to do so. They only freed the de-

velopment of American society from the retarding effect of British rule. Their political reform did not change any basic trend, but only pushed American political culture along its natural direction of development. British society, of which American society was an offshoot, had been moving for a long time in the direction of representative democracy. And prior to the War of Independence the Americans were already practicing a significant degree of representative democracy in the colonial assemblies. The political system established by the Constitution was modeled on the British system and on the colonial assemblies. With major alterations, to be sure—there is no doubt that the Founding Fathers took a very important step. But it was a step along the road that the English-speaking world was already traveling. The proof is that Britain and all of its colonies that were populated predominantly by people of British descent ended up with systems of representative democracy essentially similar to that of the United States. If the Founding Fathers had lost their nerve and declined to sign the Declaration of Independence, our way of life today would not have been significantly different. Maybe we would have had somewhat closer ties to Britain, and would have had a Parliament and Prime Minister instead of a Congress and President. No big deal. Thus the American Revolution provides not a counterexample to our principles but a good illustration of them.

110. Still, one has to use common sense in applying the principles. They are expressed in imprecise language that allows latitude for interpretation, and exceptions to them can be found. So we present these principles not as inviolable laws but as rules of thumb, or guides to thinking, that may provide a partial antidote to naïve ideas about the future of society. The principles should be borne constantly in mind, and whenever one reaches a conclusion that conflicts with them one should carefully reexamine one's thinking and retain the conclusion only if one has good, solid reasons for doing so.

Industrial-Technological Society Cannot Be Reformed

111. The foregoing principles help to show how hopelessly difficult it would be to reform the industrial system in such a way as to prevent it from progressively narrowing our sphere of freedom. There has been a consistent tendency, going back at least to the Industrial Revolution, for technology to strengthen the system at a high cost in individual freedom

and local autonomy. Hence any change designed to protect freedom from technology would be contrary to a fundamental trend in the development of our society. Consequently, such a change either would be a transitory one—soon swamped by the tide of history—or, if large enough to be permanent, would alter the nature of our whole society. This by the first and second principles. Moreover, since society would be altered in a way that could not be predicted in advance (third principle) there would be great risk. Changes large enough to make a lasting difference in favor of freedom would not be initiated because it would be realized that they would gravely disrupt the system. So any attempts at reform would be too timid to be effective. Even if changes large enough to make a lasting difference were initiated, they would be retracted when their disruptive effects became apparent. Thus, permanent changes in favor of freedom could be brought about only by persons prepared to accept radical, dangerous and unpredictable alteration of the entire system. In other words, by revolutionaries, not reformers.

112. People anxious to rescue freedom without sacrificing the supposed benefits of technology will suggest naïve schemes for some new form of society that would reconcile freedom with technology. Apart from the fact that people who make such suggestions seldom propose any practical means by which the new form of society could be set up in the first place, it follows from the fourth principle that even if the new form of society could once be established, it either would collapse or would give results very different from those expected.

113. So even on very general grounds it seems highly improbable that any way of changing society could be found that would reconcile freedom with modern technology. In the next few sections we will give more specific reasons for concluding that freedom and technological progress are incompatible.

Restriction of Freedom is Unavoidable in Industrial Society

114. As explained in paragraphs 65–67, 70–73, modern man is strapped down by a network of rules and regulations, and his fate depends on the actions of persons remote from him whose decisions he cannot influence. This is not accidental or a result of the arbitrariness of arrogant bureaucrats. It is necessary and inevitable in any technologically advanced society. The system *has to* regulate human behavior closely in

order to function. At work, people have to do what they are told to do, when they are told to do it and in the way they are told to do it, otherwise production would be thrown into chaos. Bureaucracies *have to* be run according to rigid rules. To allow any substantial personal discretion to lower-level bureaucrats would disrupt the system and lead to charges of unfairness due to differences in the way individual bureaucrats exercised their discretion. It is true that some restrictions on our freedom could be eliminated, but *generally speaking* the regulation of our lives by large organizations is necessary for the functioning of industrial-technological society. The result is a sense of powerlessness on the part of the average person. It may be, however, that formal regulations will tend increasingly to be replaced by psychological tools that make us want to do what the system requires of us. (Propaganda,[31] educational techniques, "mental health" programs, etc.)

115. The system *has to* force people to behave in ways that are increasingly remote from the natural pattern of human behavior. For example, the system needs scientists, mathematicians and engineers. It can't function without them. So heavy pressure is put on children to excel in these fields. It isn't natural for an adolescent human being to spend the bulk of his time sitting at a desk absorbed in study.[32] A normal adolescent wants to spend his time in active contact with the real world. Among primitive peoples the things that children are trained to do tend to be in reasonable harmony with natural human impulses. Among the American Indians, for example, boys were trained in active outdoor pursuits—just the sort of things that boys like. But in our society children are pushed into studying technical subjects, which most do grudgingly.

116. Because of the constant pressure that the system exerts to modify human behavior, there is a gradual increase in the number of people who cannot or will not adjust to society's requirements: welfare leeches, youth-gang members, cultists, anti-government rebels, radical environmentalist saboteurs, dropouts and resisters of various kinds.

117. In any technologically advanced society the individual's fate *must* depend on decisions that he personally cannot influence to any great extent. A technological society cannot be broken down into small, autonomous communities, because production depends on the cooperation of very large numbers of people and machines. Such a society *must* be highly organized and decisions *have to* be made that affect very large num-

bers of people. When a decision affects, say, a million people, then each of the affected individuals has, on the average, only a one-millionth share in making the decision. What usually happens in practice is that decisions are made by public officials or corporation executives, or by technical specialists, but even when the public votes on a decision the number of voters ordinarily is too large for the vote of any one individual to be significant.[33] Thus most individuals are unable to influence measurably the major decisions that affect their lives. There is no conceivable way to remedy this in a technologically advanced society. The system tries to "solve" this problem by using propaganda to make people *want* the decisions that have been made for them, but even if this "solution" were completely successful in making people feel better, it would be demeaning.

118. Conservatives and some others advocate more "local autonomy." Local communities once did have autonomy, but such autonomy becomes less and less possible as local communities become more and more enmeshed with and dependent on large-scale systems like public utilities, computer networks, highway systems, the mass communications media and the modern health-care system. Also operating against autonomy is the fact that technology applied in one location often affects people at other locations far away. Thus pesticide or chemical use near a creek may contaminate the water supply hundreds of miles downstream, and the greenhouse effect affects the whole world.

119. The system does not and cannot exist to satisfy human needs. Instead, it is human behavior that has to be modified to fit the needs of the system. This has nothing to do with the political or social ideology that may pretend to guide the technological system. It is not the fault of capitalism and it is not the fault of socialism. It is the fault of technology, because the system is guided not by ideology but by technical necessity.[34] Of course, the system does satisfy many human needs, but generally speaking it does this only to the extent that it is to the advantage of the system to do it. It is the needs of the system that are paramount, not those of the human being. For example, the system provides people with food because the system couldn't function if everyone starved; it attends to people's psychological needs whenever it can *conveniently* do so, because it couldn't function if too many people became depressed or rebellious. But the system, for good, solid, practical reasons, must exert constant pressure on people to mold their behavior to the needs of the system. Too

much waste accumulating? The government, the media, the educational system, environmentalists, everyone inundates us with a mass of propaganda about recycling. Need more technical personnel? A chorus of voices exhorts kids to study science. No one stops to ask whether it is inhumane to force adolescents to spend the bulk of their time studying subjects that most of them hate. When skilled workers are put out of a job by technical advances and have to undergo "retraining," no one asks whether it is humiliating for them to be pushed around in this way. It is simply taken for granted that everyone must bow to technical necessity. And for good reason: If human needs were put before technical necessity there would be economic problems, unemployment, shortages or worse. The concept of "mental health" in our society is defined largely by the extent to which an individual behaves in accord with the needs of the system and does so without showing signs of stress.

120. Efforts to make room for a sense of purpose and for autonomy within the system are no better than a joke. For example, one company, instead of having each of its employees assemble only one section of a telephone book, had each assemble a whole telephone book, and this was supposed to give them a sense of purpose and achievement. Some companies have tried to give their employees more autonomy in their work, but for practical reasons this usually can be done only to a very limited extent, and in any case employees are never given autonomy as to ultimate goals—their "autonomous" efforts can never be directed toward goals that they select personally, but only toward their employer's goals, such as the survival and growth of the company. Any company would soon go out of business if it permitted its employees to act otherwise. Similarly, in any enterprise within a socialist system, workers must direct their efforts toward the goals of the enterprise, otherwise the enterprise will not serve its purpose as part of the system. Once again, for purely technical reasons it is not possible for most individuals or small groups to have much autonomy in industrial society. Even the small-business owner commonly has only limited autonomy. Apart from the necessity of government regulation, he is restricted by the fact that he must fit into the economic system and conform to its requirements. For instance, when someone develops a new technology, the small-business person often has to use that technology whether he wants to or not, in order to remain competitive.

The "Bad" Parts of Technology Cannot Be Separated from the "Good" Parts

121. A further reason why industrial society cannot be reformed in favor of freedom is that modern technology is a unified system in which all parts are dependent on one another. You can't get rid of the "bad" parts of technology and retain only the "good" parts. Take modern medicine, for example. Progress in medical science depends on progress in chemistry, physics, biology, computer science and other fields. Advanced medical treatments require expensive, high-tech equipment that can be made available only by a technologically progressive, economically rich society. Clearly you can't have much progress in medicine without the whole technological system and everything that goes with it.

122. Even if medical progress could be maintained without the rest of the technological system, it would by itself bring certain evils. Suppose for example that a cure for diabetes is discovered. People with a genetic tendency to diabetes will then be able to survive and reproduce as well as anyone else. Natural selection against genes for diabetes will cease and such genes will spread throughout the population. (This may be occurring to some extent already, since diabetes, while not curable, can be controlled through the use of insulin.) The same thing will happen with many other diseases susceptibility to which is affected by genetic factors (e.g., childhood cancer), resulting in massive genetic degradation of the population.[35] The only solution will be some sort of eugenics program or extensive genetic engineering of human beings, so that man in the future will no longer be a creation of nature, or of chance, or of God (depending on your religious or philosophical opinions), but a manufactured product.

123. If you think that big government interferes in your life too much *now*, just wait till the government starts regulating the genetic constitution of your children. Such regulation will inevitably follow the introduction of genetic engineering of human beings, because the consequences of unregulated genetic engineering would be disastrous.[36]

124. The usual response to such concerns is to talk about "medical ethics." But a code of ethics would not serve to protect freedom in the face of medical progress; it would only make matters worse. A code of ethics applicable to genetic engineering would be in effect a means of regulating the genetic constitution of human beings. Somebody (probably the upper middle class, mostly) would decide that such and such applications of ge-

netic engineering were "ethical" and others were not, so that in effect they would be imposing their own values on the genetic constitution of the population at large. Even if a code of ethics were chosen on a completely democratic basis, the majority would be imposing their own values on any minorities who might have a different idea of what constituted an "ethical" use of genetic engineering. The only code of ethics that would truly protect freedom would be one that prohibited *any* genetic engineering of human beings, and you can be sure that no such code will ever be applied in a technological society. No code that reduced genetic engineering to a minor role could stand up for long, because the temptation presented by the immense power of biotechnology would be irresistible, especially since to the majority of people many of its applications will seem obviously and unequivocally good (eliminating physical and mental diseases, giving people the abilities they need to get along in today's world). Inevitably, genetic engineering will be used extensively, but only in ways consistent with the needs of the industrial-technological system.

Technology is a More Powerful Social Force than the Aspiration for Freedom

125. It is not possible to make a *lasting* compromise between technology and freedom, because technology is by far the more powerful social force and continually encroaches on freedom through *repeated* compromises. Imagine the case of two neighbors, each of whom at the outset owns the same amount of land, but one of whom is more powerful than the other. The powerful one demands a piece of the other's land. The weak one refuses. The powerful one says, "Okay, let's compromise. Give me half of what I asked." The weak one has little choice but to give in. Some time later the powerful neighbor demands another piece of land, again there is a compromise, and so forth. By forcing a long series of compromises on the weaker man, the powerful one eventually gets all of his land. So it goes in the conflict between technology and freedom.

126. Let us explain why technology is a more powerful social force than the aspiration for freedom.

127. A technological advance that appears not to threaten freedom often turns out to threaten it very seriously later on. For example, consider motorized transport. A walking man formerly could go where he pleased, go at his own pace without observing any traffic regulations, and was in-

dependent of technological support systems. When motor vehicles were introduced they appeared to increase man's freedom. They took no freedom away from the walking man, no one had to have an automobile if he didn't want one, and anyone who did choose to buy an automobile could travel much faster and farther than a walking man. But the introduction of motorized transport soon changed society in such a way as to restrict greatly man's freedom of locomotion. When automobiles became numerous, it was found necessary to regulate their use extensively. In a car, especially in densely populated areas, one cannot just go where one likes at one's own pace; one's movement is governed by the flow of traffic and by various traffic laws. One is tied down by various obligations: license requirements, driver test, renewing registration, insurance, maintenance required for safety, monthly payments on purchase price. Moreover, the use of motorized transport is no longer optional. Since the introduction of motorized transport the arrangement of our cities has changed in such a way that the majority of people no longer live within walking distance of their place of employment, shopping areas and recreational opportunities, so that they *have to* depend on the automobile for transportation. Or else they must use public transportation, in which case they have even less control over their own movement than when driving a car. Even the walker's freedom is now greatly restricted. In the city he continually has to stop to wait for traffic lights that are designed mainly to serve auto traffic. In the country, motor traffic makes it dangerous and unpleasant to walk along the highway. (Note this important point that we have just illustrated with the case of motorized transport: When a new item of technology is introduced as an option that an individual can accept or not as he chooses, it does not necessarily *remain* optional. In many cases the new technology changes society in such a way that people eventually find themselves *forced* to use it.)

128. While technological progress *as a whole* continually narrows our sphere of freedom, each new technical advance *considered by itself* appears to be desirable. Electricity, indoor plumbing, rapid long-distance communications… how could one argue against any of these things, or against any other of the innumerable technical advances that have made modern society? It would have been absurd to resist the introduction of the telephone, for example. It offered many advantages and no disadvantages. Yet, as we explained in paragraphs 59–76, all these technical advances taken

together have created a world in which the average man's fate is no longer in his own hands or in the hands of his neighbors and friends, but in those of politicians, corporation executives and remote, anonymous technicians and bureaucrats whom he as an individual has no power to influence.[37] The same process will continue in the future. Take genetic engineering, for example. Few people will resist the introduction of a genetic technique that eliminates a hereditary disease. It does no apparent harm and prevents much suffering. Yet a large number of genetic improvements taken together will make the human being into an engineered product rather than a free creation of chance (or of God, or whatever, depending on your religious beliefs).

129. Another reason why technology is such a powerful social force is that, within the context of a given society, technological progress marches in only one direction; it can never be reversed. Once a technical innovation has been introduced, people usually become dependent on it, so that they can never again do without it, unless it is replaced by some still more advanced innovation. Not only do people become dependent as individuals on a new item of technology, but, even more, the system as a whole becomes dependent on it. (Imagine what would happen to the system today if computers, for example, were eliminated.) Thus the system can move in only one direction, toward greater technologization. Technology repeatedly forces freedom to take a step back but technology can never take a step back—short of the overthrow of the whole technological system.

130. Technology advances with great rapidity and threatens freedom at many different points at the same time (crowding, rules and regulations, increasing dependence of individuals on large organizations, propaganda and other psychological techniques, genetic engineering, invasion of privacy through surveillance devices and computers, etc.). To hold back any *one* of the threats to freedom would require a long and difficult social struggle. Those who want to protect freedom are overwhelmed by the sheer number of new attacks and the rapidity with which they develop, hence they become apathetic and no longer resist. To fight each of the threats separately would be futile. Success can be hoped for only by fighting the technological system as a whole; but that is revolution, not reform.

131. Technicians (we use this term in its broad sense to describe all those who perform a specialized task that requires training) tend to be so involved in their work (their surrogate activity) that when a conflict arises

between their technical work and freedom, they almost always decide in favor of their technical work. This is obvious in the case of scientists, but it also appears elsewhere: Educators, humanitarian groups, conservation organizations do not hesitate to use propaganda[38] or other psychological techniques to help them achieve their laudable ends. Corporations and government agencies, when they find it useful, do not hesitate to collect information about individuals without regard to their privacy. Law-enforcement agencies are frequently inconvenienced by the constitutional rights of suspects and often of completely innocent persons, and they do whatever they can do legally (or sometimes illegally) to restrict or circumvent those rights. Most of these educators, government officials and law officers believe in freedom, privacy and constitutional rights, but when these conflict with their work, they usually feel that their work is more important.

132. It is well known that people generally work better and more persistently when striving for a reward than when attempting to avoid a punishment or negative outcome. Scientists and other technicians are motivated mainly by the rewards they get through their work. But those who oppose technological invasions of freedom are working to avoid a negative outcome, consequently there are few who work persistently and well at this discouraging task. If reformers ever achieved a signal victory that seemed to set up a solid barrier against further erosion of freedom through technical progress, most would tend to relax and turn their attention to more agreeable pursuits. But the scientists would remain busy in their laboratories, and technology as it progressed would find ways, in spite of any barriers, to exert more and more control over individuals and make them always more dependent on the system.

133. No social arrangements, whether laws, institutions, customs, or ethical codes, can provide permanent protection against technology. History shows that all social arrangements are transitory; they all change or break down eventually. But technological advances are permanent within the context of a given civilization. Suppose for example that it were possible to arrive at some social arrangement that would prevent genetic engineering from being applied to human beings, or prevent it from being applied in such a way as to threaten freedom and dignity. Still the technology would remain, waiting. Sooner or later the social arrangement would break down. Probably sooner, given the pace of change in our so-

ciety. Then genetic engineering would begin to invade our sphere of freedom, and this invasion would be irreversible (short of a breakdown of technological civilization itself). Any illusions about achieving anything permanent through social arrangements should be dispelled by what is currently [as of 1995] happening with environmental legislation. A few years ago it seemed that there were secure legal barriers preventing at least *some* of the worst forms of environmental degradation. A change in the political wind, and those barriers begin to crumble.

134. For all of the foregoing reasons, technology is a more powerful social force than the aspiration for freedom. But this statement requires an important qualification. It appears that during the next several decades the industrial-technological system will be undergoing severe stresses due to economic and environmental problems, and especially due to problems of human behavior (alienation, rebellion, hostility, a variety of social and psychological difficulties). We hope that the stresses through which the system is likely to pass will cause it to break down, or at least will weaken it sufficiently so that a revolution against it becomes possible. If such a revolution occurs and is successful, then at that particular moment the aspiration for freedom will have proven more powerful than technology.

135. In paragraph 125 we used an analogy of a weak neighbor who is left destitute by a strong neighbor who takes all his land by forcing on him a series of compromises. But suppose now that the strong neighbor gets sick, so that he is unable to defend himself. The weak neighbor can force the strong one to give him his land back, or he can kill him. If he lets the strong man survive and only forces him to give the land back, he is a fool, because when the strong man gets well he will again take all the land for himself. The only sensible alternative for the weaker man is to kill the strong one while he has the chance. In the same way, while the industrial system is sick we must destroy it. If we compromise with it and let it recover from its sickness, it will eventually wipe out all of our freedom.

Simpler Social Problems Have Proved Intractable

136. If anyone still imagines that it would be possible to reform the system in such a way as to protect freedom from technology, let him consider how clumsily and for the most part unsuccessfully our society has dealt with other social problems that are far more simple and straightfor-

ward. Among other things, the system has failed to stop environmental degradation, political corruption, drug trafficking or domestic abuse.

137. Take our environmental problems, for example. Here the conflict of values is straightforward: economic expedience now versus saving some of our natural resources for our grandchildren.[39] But on this subject we get only a lot of blather and obfuscation from the people who have power, and nothing like a clear, consistent line of action, and we keep on piling up environmental problems that our grandchildren will have to live with. Attempts to resolve the environmental issue consist of struggles and compromises between different factions, some of which are ascendant at one moment, others at another moment. The line of struggle changes with the shifting currents of public opinion. This is not a rational process, nor is it one that is likely to lead to a timely and successful solution to the problem. Major social problems, if they get "solved" at all, rarely or never are solved through any rational, comprehensive plan. They just work themselves out through a process in which various competing groups pursuing their own (usually short-term) self-interest[40] arrive (mainly by luck) at some more or less stable modus vivendi. In fact, the principles we formulated in paragraphs 100–06 make it seem doubtful that rational, long-term social planning can *ever* be successful.

138. Thus it is clear that the human race has at best a very limited capacity for solving even relatively straightforward social problems. How then is it going to solve the far more difficult and subtle problem of reconciling freedom with technology? Technology presents clear-cut material advantages, whereas freedom is an abstraction that means different things to different people, and its loss is easily obscured by propaganda and fancy talk.

139. And note this important difference: It is conceivable that our environmental problems (for example) may some day be settled through a rational, comprehensive plan, but if this happens it will be only because it is in the long-term interest of the system to solve these problems. But it is *not* in the interest of the system to preserve freedom or small-group autonomy. On the contrary, it is in the interest of the system to bring human behavior under control to the greatest possible extent.[41] Thus, while practical considerations may eventually force the system to take a rational, prudent approach to environmental problems, equally practical considerations will force the system to regulate human behavior ever more closely

(preferably by indirect means that will disguise the encroachment on freedom). This isn't just our opinion. Eminent social scientists (e.g., James Q. Wilson) have stressed the importance of "socializing" people more effectively.

Revolution is Easier than Reform

140. We hope we have convinced the reader that the system cannot be reformed in such a way as to reconcile freedom with technology. The only way out is to dispense with the industrial-technological system altogether. This implies revolution, not necessarily an armed uprising, but certainly a radical and fundamental change in the nature of society.

141. People tend to assume that because a revolution involves a much greater change than reform does, it is more difficult to bring about than reform is. Actually, under certain circumstances, revolution is much easier than reform. The reason is that a revolutionary movement can inspire an intensity of commitment that a reform movement cannot inspire. A reform movement merely offers to solve a particular social problem. A revolutionary movement offers to solve all problems at one stroke and create a whole new world; it provides the kind of ideal for which people will take great risks and make great sacrifices. For this reason it would be much easier to overthrow the whole technological system than to put effective, permanent restraints on the development or application of any one segment of technology, such as genetic engineering, for example. Not many people will devote themselves with single-minded passion to imposing and maintaining restraints on genetic engineering, but under suitable conditions large numbers of people may devote themselves passionately to a revolution against the industrial-technological system. As we noted in paragraph 132, reformers seeking to limit certain aspects of technology would be working to avoid a negative outcome. But revolutionaries work to gain a powerful reward—fulfillment of their revolutionary vision—and therefore work harder and more persistently than reformers do.

142. Reform is always restrained by the fear of painful consequences if changes go too far. But once a revolutionary fever has taken hold of a society, people are willing to undergo unlimited hardships for the sake of their revolution. This was clearly shown in the French and Russian Revolutions. It may be that in such cases only a minority of the population is really committed to the revolution, but this minority is sufficiently large

and active so that it becomes the dominant force in society. We will have more to say about revolution in paragraphs 180–205.

Control of Human Behavior

143. Since the beginning of civilization, organized societies have had to put pressures on human beings for the sake of the functioning of the social organism. The kinds of pressures vary greatly from one society to another. Some of the pressures are physical (poor diet, excessive labor, environmental pollution), some are psychological (noise, crowding, forcing human behavior into the mold that society requires). In the past, human nature has been approximately constant, or at any rate has varied only within certain bounds. Consequently, societies have been able to push people only up to certain limits. When the limit of human endurance has been passed, things start going wrong: rebellion, or crime, or corruption, or evasion of work, or depression and other mental problems, or an elevated death rate, or a declining birth rate or something else, so that either the society breaks down, or its functioning becomes too inefficient and it is (quickly or gradually, through conquest, attrition or evolution) replaced by some more efficient form of society.[42]

144. Thus human nature has in the past put certain limits on the development of societies. People could be pushed only so far and no farther. But today this may be changing, because modern technology is developing ways of modifying human beings.

145. Imagine a society that subjects people to conditions that make them terribly unhappy, then gives them drugs to take away their unhappiness. Science fiction? It is already happening to some extent in our own society. It is well known that the rate of clinical depression has been greatly increasing in recent decades. We believe that this is due to disruption of the power process, as explained in paragraphs 59–76. But even if we are wrong, the increasing rate of depression is certainly the result of *some* conditions that exist in today's society. Instead of removing the conditions that make people depressed, modern society gives them antidepressant drugs. In effect, antidepressants are a means of modifying an individual's internal state in such a way as to enable him to tolerate social conditions that he would otherwise find intolerable. (Yes, we know that depression is often of purely genetic origin. We are referring here to those cases in which environment plays the predominant role.)

146. Drugs that affect the mind are only one example of the methods of controlling human behavior that modern society is developing. Let us look at some of the other methods.

147. To start with, there are the techniques of surveillance. Hidden video cameras are now used in most stores and in many other places, computers are used to collect and process vast amounts of information about individuals. Information so obtained greatly increases the effectiveness of physical coercion (i.e., law enforcement).[43] Then there are the methods of propaganda, for which the mass communications media provide effective vehicles. Efficient techniques have been developed for winning elections, selling products, influencing public opinion. The entertainment industry serves as an important psychological tool of the system, possibly even when it is dishing out large amounts of sex and violence. Entertainment provides modern man with an essential means of escape. While absorbed in television, videos, etc., he can forget stress, anxiety, frustration, dissatisfaction. Many primitive peoples, when they don't have any work to do, are quite content to sit for hours at a time doing nothing at all, because they are at peace with themselves and their world. But most modern people must be constantly occupied or entertained, otherwise they get "bored," i.e., they get fidgety, uneasy, irritable.[44]

148. Other techniques strike deeper than the foregoing. Education is no longer a simple affair of paddling a kid's behind when he doesn't know his lessons and patting him on the head when he does know them. It is becoming a scientific technique for controlling the child's development. Sylvan Learning Centers, for example, have had great success in motivating children to study, and psychological techniques are also used with more or less success in many conventional schools. "Parenting" techniques that are taught to parents are designed to make children accept the fundamental values of the system and behave in ways that the system finds desirable. "Mental health" programs, "intervention" techniques, psychotherapy and so forth are ostensibly designed to benefit individuals, but in practice they usually serve as methods for inducing individuals to think and behave as the system requires. (There is no contradiction here; an individual whose attitudes or behavior bring him into conflict with the system is up against a force that is too powerful for him to conquer or escape from, hence he is likely to suffer from stress, frustration, defeat. His path will be much easier if he thinks and behaves as the system requires. In that

sense the system is acting for the benefit of the individual when it brainwashes him into conformity.) Child abuse in its gross and obvious forms is disapproved in most if not all cultures. Tormenting a child for a trivial reason or no reason at all is something that appalls almost everyone. But many psychologists interpret the concept of abuse much more broadly. Is spanking, when used as part of a rational and consistent system of discipline, a form of abuse? The question will ultimately be decided by whether or not spanking tends to produce behavior that makes a person fit in well with the existing system of society. In practice, the word "abuse" tends to be interpreted to include any method of child-rearing that produces behavior inconvenient for the system. Thus, when they go beyond the prevention of obvious, senseless cruelty, programs for preventing "child abuse" are directed toward the control of human behavior on behalf of the system.

149. Presumably, research will continue to increase the effectiveness of psychological techniques for controlling human behavior. But we think it is unlikely that psychological techniques alone will be sufficient to adjust human beings to the kind of society that technology is creating. Biological methods probably will have to be used. We have already mentioned the use of drugs in this connection. Neurology may provide other avenues for modifying the human mind. Genetic engineering of human beings is already beginning to occur in the form of "gene therapy," and there is no reason to assume that such methods will not eventually be used to modify those aspects of the body that affect mental functioning.

150. As we mentioned in paragraph 134, industrial society seems likely to be entering a period of severe stress, due in part to problems of human behavior and in part to economic and environmental problems. And a considerable proportion of the system's economic and environmental problems result from the way human beings behave. Alienation, low self-esteem, depression, hostility, rebellion; children who won't study, youth gangs, illegal drug use, rape, child abuse, other crimes, unsafe sex, teen pregnancy, population growth, political corruption, race hatred, ethnic rivalry, bitter ideological conflict (e.g., pro-choice vs. pro-life), political extremism, terrorism, sabotage, anti-government groups, hate groups. All these threaten the very survival of the system. The system will therefore be *forced* to use every practical means of controlling human behavior.

151. The social disruption that we see today is certainly not the result of mere chance. It can only be a result of the conditions of life that

the system imposes on people. (We have argued that the most important of these conditions is disruption of the power process.) If the system succeeds in imposing sufficient control over human behavior to ensure its own survival, a new watershed in human history will have been passed. Whereas formerly the limits of human endurance have imposed limits on the development of societies (as we explained in paragraphs 143, 144), industrial-technological society will be able to pass those limits by modifying human beings, whether by psychological methods or biological methods or both. In the future, social systems will not be adjusted to suit the needs of human beings. Instead, human beings will be adjusted to suit the needs of the system.[45]

152. Generally speaking, technological control over human behavior will probably not be introduced with a totalitarian intention or even through a conscious desire to restrict human freedom.[46] Each new step in the assertion of control over the human mind will be taken as a rational response to a problem that faces society, such as curing alcoholism, reducing the crime rate or inducing young people to study science and engineering. In many cases, there will be a humanitarian justification. For example, when a psychiatrist prescribes an antidepressant for a depressed patient, he is clearly doing that individual a favor. It would be inhumane to withhold the drug from someone who needs it. When parents send their children to Sylvan Learning Centers to have them manipulated into becoming enthusiastic about their studies, they do so from concern for their children's welfare. It may be that some of these parents wish that one didn't have to have specialized training to get a job and that their kid didn't have to be brainwashed into becoming a computer nerd. But what can they do? They can't change society, and their child may be unemployable if he doesn't have certain skills. So they send him to Sylvan.

153. Thus control over human behavior will be introduced not by a calculated decision of the authorities but through a process of social evolution (*rapid* evolution, however). The process will be impossible to resist, because each advance, considered by itself, will appear to be beneficial, or at least the evil involved in making the advance will seem to be less than that which would result from not making it. (See paragraph 127.) Propaganda for example is used for many good purposes, such as discouraging child abuse or race hatred.[47] Sex education is obviously useful, yet the effect of sex education (to the extent that it is successful) is to take the shap-

ing of sexual attitudes away from the family and put it into the hands of the state as represented by the public school system.

154. Suppose a biological trait is discovered that increases the likelihood that a child will grow up to be a criminal, and suppose some sort of gene therapy can remove this trait.[48] Of course, most parents whose children possess the trait will have them undergo the therapy. It would be inhumane to do otherwise, since the child would probably have a miserable life if he grew up to be a criminal. But many or most primitive societies have a low crime rate in comparison with that of our society, even though they have neither high-tech methods of child-rearing nor harsh systems of punishment. Since there is no reason to suppose that more modern men than primitive men have innate predatory tendencies, the high crime rate of our society must be due to the pressures that modern conditions put on people, to which many cannot or will not adjust. Thus a treatment designed to remove potential criminal tendencies is at least in part a way of re-engineering people so that they suit the requirements of the system.

155. Our society tends to regard as a "sickness" any mode of thought or behavior that is inconvenient for the system, and this is plausible, because when an individual doesn't fit into the system it causes pain to the individual as well as problems for the system. Thus the manipulation of an individual to adjust him to the system is seen as a "cure" for a "sickness" and therefore as good.

156. In paragraph 127 we pointed out that if the use of a new item of technology is *initially* optional, it does not necessarily *remain* optional, because the new technology tends to change society in such a way that it becomes difficult or impossible for an individual to function without using that technology. This applies also to the technology of human behavior. In a world in which most children are put through a program to make them enthusiastic about studying, a parent will almost be forced to put his kid through such a program, because if he does not, then the kid will grow up to be, comparatively speaking, an ignoramus and therefore unemployable. Or suppose a biological treatment is discovered that, without undesirable side-effects, will greatly reduce the psychological stress from which so many people suffer in our society. If large numbers of people choose to undergo the treatment, then the general level of stress in society will be reduced, so that it will be possible for the system to increase the stress-producing pressures. This will lead more people to undergo the treatment;

and so forth, so that eventually the pressures may become so heavy that few people will be able to survive without undergoing the stress-reducing treatment. In fact, something like this seems to have happened already with one of our society's most important psychological tools for enabling people to reduce (or at least temporarily escape from) stress, namely, mass entertainment (see paragraph 147). Our use of mass entertainment is "optional": No law requires us to watch television, listen to the radio, read magazines. Yet mass entertainment is a means of escape and stress-reduction on which most of us have become dependent. Everyone complains about the trashiness of television, but almost everyone watches it. A few have kicked the TV habit, but it would be a rare person who could get along today without using *any* form of mass entertainment. (Yet until quite recently in human history most people got along very nicely with no other entertainment than that which each local community created for itself.) Without the entertainment industry the system probably would not have been able to get away with putting as much stress-producing pressure on us as it does.

157. Assuming that industrial society survives, it is likely that technology will eventually acquire something approaching complete control over human behavior. It has been established beyond any rational doubt that human thought and behavior have a largely biological basis. As experimenters have demonstrated, feelings such as hunger, pleasure, anger and fear can be turned on and off by electrical stimulation of appropriate parts of the brain. Memories can be destroyed by damaging parts of the brain or they can be brought to the surface by electrical stimulation. Hallucinations can be induced or moods changed by drugs. There may or may not be an immaterial human soul, but if there is one it clearly is less powerful than the biological mechanisms of human behavior. For if that were not the case then researchers would not be able so easily to manipulate human feelings and behavior with drugs and electrical currents.

158. It presumably would be impractical for all people to have electrodes inserted in their heads so that they could be controlled by the authorities. But the fact that human thoughts and feelings are so open to biological intervention shows that the problem of controlling human behavior is mainly a technical problem; a problem of neurons, hormones and complex molecules; the kind of problem that is accessible to scientific attack. Given the outstanding record of our society in solving technical

problems, it is overwhelmingly probable that great advances will be made in the control of human behavior.

159. Will public resistance prevent the introduction of technological control of human behavior? It certainly would if an attempt were made to introduce such control all at once. But since technological control will be introduced through a long sequence of small advances, there will be no rational and effective public resistance. (See paragraphs 127, 132, 153.)

160. To those who think that all this sounds like science fiction, we point out that yesterday's science fiction is today's fact. The Industrial Revolution has radically altered man's environment and way of life, and it is only to be expected that as technology is increasingly applied to the human body and mind, man himself will be altered as radically as his environment and way of life have been.

Human Race at a Crossroads

161. But we have gotten ahead of our story. It is one thing to develop in the laboratory a series of psychological or biological techniques for manipulating human behavior and quite another to integrate these techniques into a functioning social system. The latter problem is the more difficult of the two. For example, while the techniques of educational psychology doubtless work quite well in the "lab schools" where they are developed, it is not necessarily easy to apply them effectively throughout our educational system. We all know what many of our schools are like. The teachers are too busy [as of 1995] taking knives and guns away from the kids to subject them to the latest techniques for making them into computer nerds. Thus, in spite of all its technical advances relating to human behavior, the system to date has not been impressively successful in controlling human beings. The people whose behavior is fairly well under the control of the system are those of the type that might be called "bourgeois." But there are growing numbers of people who in one way or another are rebels against the system: welfare leeches, youth gangs, cultists, satanists, Nazis, radical environmentalists, militiamen, etc.

162. The system is currently engaged in a desperate struggle to overcome certain problems that threaten its survival, among which the problems of human behavior are the most important. If the system succeeds in acquiring sufficient control over human behavior quickly enough, it will probably survive. Otherwise it will break down. We think the issue will

most likely be resolved within the next several decades, say forty to a hundred years.

163. Suppose the system survives the crisis of the next several decades. By that time it will have to have solved, or at least brought under control, the principal problems that confront it, in particular that of "socializing" human beings; that is, making people sufficiently docile so that their behavior no longer threatens the system. That being accomplished, it does not appear that there would be any further obstacle to the development of technology, and it would presumably advance toward its logical conclusion, which is complete control over everything on Earth, including human beings and all other important organisms. The system may become a unitary, monolithic organization, or it may be more or less fragmented and consist of a number of organizations coexisting in a relationship that includes elements of both cooperation and competition, just as today the government, the corporations and other large organizations both cooperate and compete with one another. Human freedom mostly will have vanished, because individuals and small groups will be impotent vis-à-vis large organizations armed with supertechnology and an arsenal of advanced psychological and biological tools for manipulating human beings, besides instruments of surveillance and physical coercion. Only a small number of people will have any real power, and even these probably will have only very limited freedom, because their behavior too will be regulated; just as today our politicians and corporation executives can retain their positions of power only as long as their behavior remains within certain fairly narrow limits.

164. Don't imagine that the system will stop developing further techniques for controlling human beings and nature once the crisis of the next few decades is over and increasing control is no longer necessary for the system's survival. On the contrary, once the hard times are over the system will increase its control over people and nature more rapidly, because it will no longer be hampered by difficulties of the kind that it is currently experiencing. Survival is not the principal motive for extending control. As we explained in paragraphs 87–90, technicians and scientists carry on their work largely as a surrogate activity; that is, they satisfy their need for power by solving technical problems. They will continue to do this with unabated enthusiasm, and among the most interesting and challenging problems for them to solve will be those of understanding the human

body and mind and intervening in their development. For the "good of humanity," of course.

165. But suppose on the other hand that the stresses of the coming decades prove to be too much for the system. If the system breaks down there may be a period of chaos, a "time of troubles" such as those that history has recorded at various epochs in the past. It is impossible to predict what would emerge from such a time of troubles, but at any rate the human race would be given a new chance. The greatest danger is that industrial society may begin to reconstitute itself within the first few years after the breakdown. Certainly there will be many people (power-hungry types especially) who will be anxious to get the factories running again.

166. Therefore two tasks confront those who hate the servitude to which the industrial system is reducing the human race. First, we must work to heighten the social stresses within the system so as to increase the likelihood that it will break down or be weakened sufficiently so that a revolution against it becomes possible. Second, it is necessary to develop and propagate an ideology that opposes technology and the industrial system. Such an ideology can become the basis for a revolution against industrial society if and when the system becomes sufficiently weakened. And such an ideology will help to ensure that, if and when industrial society breaks down, its remnants will be smashed beyond repair, so that the system cannot be reconstituted. The factories should be destroyed, technical books burned, etc.

Human Suffering

167. The industrial system will not break down purely as a result of revolutionary action. It will not be vulnerable to revolutionary attack unless its own internal problems of development lead it into very serious difficulties. So if the system breaks down it will do so either spontaneously, or through a process that is in part spontaneous but helped along by revolutionaries. If the breakdown is sudden, many people will die, since the world has become so grossly overpopulated that it cannot even feed itself any longer without advanced technology. Even if the breakdown is gradual enough so that reduction of the population can occur more through lowering of the birth rate than through elevation of the death rate,[49] the process of de-industrialization probably will be very chaotic and involve much suffering. It is naive to think it likely that technology can be phased

out in a smoothly managed, orderly way, especially since the technophiles will fight stubbornly at every step. Is it therefore cruel to work for the breakdown of the system? Maybe, but maybe not. In the first place, revolutionaries will not be able to break the system down unless it is already in enough trouble so that there would be a good chance of its eventually breaking down by itself anyway; and the bigger the system grows, the more disastrous the consequences of its breakdown will be; so it may be that revolutionaries, by hastening the onset of the breakdown, will be reducing the extent of the disaster.

168. In the second place, one has to balance struggle and death against the loss of freedom and dignity. To many of us, freedom and dignity are more important than a long life or avoidance of physical pain. Besides, we all have to die sometime, and it may be better to die fighting for survival, or for a cause, than to live a long but empty and purposeless life.

169. In the third place, it is not at all certain that survival of the system will lead to less suffering than the breakdown of the system would. The system has already caused, and is continuing to cause, immense suffering all over the world. Ancient cultures, that for hundreds or thousands of years gave people a satisfactory relationship with each other and with their environment, have been shattered by contact with industrial society, and the result has been a whole catalog of economic, environmental, social and psychological problems. One of the effects of the intrusion of industrial society has been that over much of the world traditional controls on population have been thrown out of balance. Hence the population explosion, with all that that implies. Then there is the psychological suffering that is widespread throughout the supposedly fortunate countries of the West (see paragraphs 44, 45). No one knows [as of 1995] what will happen as a result of ozone depletion, the greenhouse effect and other environmental problems that cannot yet be foreseen. And, as nuclear proliferation has shown, new technology cannot be kept out of the hands of dictators and irresponsible Third World nations. Would you like to speculate about what Iraq or North Korea will do with genetic engineering?

170. "Oh!" say the technophiles, "Science is going to fix all that! We will conquer famine, eliminate psychological suffering, make everybody healthy and happy!" Yeah, sure. That's what they said two hundred years ago. The Industrial Revolution was supposed to eliminate poverty, make everybody happy, etc. The actual result has been quite different. The tech-

nophiles are hopelessly naive (or self-deceiving) in their understanding of social problems. They are unaware of (or choose to ignore) the fact that when large changes, even seemingly beneficial ones, are introduced into a society, they lead to a long sequence of other changes, most of which are impossible to predict (paragraph 103). The result is disruption of the society. So it is very probable that in their attempts to end poverty and disease, engineer docile, happy personalities and so forth, the technophiles will create social systems that are terribly troubled, even more so than the present one. For example, the scientists boast that they will end famine by creating new, genetically engineered food plants. But this will allow the human population to keep expanding indefinitely, and it is well known that crowding leads to increased stress and aggression. This is merely one example of the *predictable* problems that will arise. We emphasize that, as past experience has shown, technical progress will lead to other new problems that *cannot* be predicted in advance (paragraph 103). In fact, ever since the Industrial Revolution, technology has been creating new problems for society far more rapidly than it has been solving old ones. Thus it will take a long and difficult period of trial and error for the technophiles to work the bugs out of their Brave New World (if they ever do). In the meantime there will be great suffering. So it is not at all clear that the survival of industrial society would involve less suffering than the breakdown of that society would. Technology has gotten the human race into a fix from which there is not likely to be any easy escape.

The Future[50]

171. But suppose now that industrial society does survive the next several decades and that the bugs do eventually get worked out of the system, so that it functions smoothly. What kind of system will it be? We will consider several possibilities.

172. First let us postulate that the computer scientists succeed in developing intelligent machines that can do all things better than human beings can do them. In that case presumably all work will be done by vast, highly organized systems of machines and no human effort will be necessary. Either of two cases might occur. The machines might be permitted to make all of their own decisions without human oversight, or else human control over the machines might be retained.

173. If the machines are permitted to make all their own decisions

we can't make any conjecture as to the results, because it is impossible to guess how such machines might behave. We only point out that the fate of the human race would be at the mercy of the machines. It might be argued that the human race would never be foolish enough to hand over all power to the machines. But we are suggesting neither that the human race would voluntarily turn power over to the machines nor that the machines would willfully seize power. What we do suggest is that the human race might easily permit itself to drift into a position of such dependence on the machines that it would have no practical choice but to accept all of the machines' decisions. As society and the problems that face it become more and more complex and as machines become more and more intelligent, people will let machines make more and more of their decisions for them, simply because machine-made decisions will bring better results than man-made ones. Eventually a stage may be reached at which the decisions necessary to keep the system running will be so complex that human beings will be incapable of making them intelligently. At that stage the machines will be in effective control. People won't be able to just turn the machines off, because they will be so dependent on them that turning them off would amount to suicide.

174.   On the other hand, it is possible that human control over the machines may be retained. In that case the average man may have control over certain private machines of his own, such as his car or his personal computer, but control over large systems of machines will be in the hands of a tiny elite—just as it is today, but with two differences. Due to improved techniques the elite will have greater control over the masses; and because human work will no longer be necessary the masses will be superfluous, a useless burden on the system. If the elite is ruthless they may simply decide to exterminate the mass of humanity. If they are humane they may use propaganda or other psychological or biological techniques to reduce the birth rate until the mass of humanity becomes extinct, leaving the world to the elite. Or, if the elite consists of soft-hearted liberals, they may decide to play the role of good shepherds to the rest of the human race. They will see to it that everyone's physical needs are satisfied, that all children are raised under psychologically hygienic conditions, that everyone has a wholesome hobby to keep him busy, and that anyone who may become dissatisfied undergoes "treatment" to cure his "problem." Of course, life will be so purposeless that people will have to be biologically

or psychologically engineered either to remove their need for the power process or to make them "sublimate" their drive for power into some harmless hobby. These engineered human beings may be happy in such a society, but they most certainly will not be free. They will have been reduced to the status of domestic animals.

175. But suppose now that the computer scientists do not succeed in developing strong artificial intelligence, so that human work remains necessary. Even so, machines will take care of more and more of the simpler tasks so that there will be an increasing surplus of human workers at the lower levels of ability. (We see this happening already. There are many people who find it difficult or impossible to get work, because for intellectual or psychological reasons they cannot acquire the level of training necessary to make themselves useful in the present system.) On those who are employed, ever-increasing demands will be placed: They will need more and more training, more and more ability, and will have to be ever more reliable, conforming and docile, because they will be more and more like cells of a giant organism. Their tasks will be increasingly specialized, so that their work will be, in a sense, out of touch with the real world, being concentrated on one tiny slice of reality. The system will have to use any means that it can, whether psychological or biological, to engineer people to be docile, to have the abilities that the system requires and to "sublimate" their drive for power into some specialized task. But the statement that the people of such a society will have to be docile may require qualification. The society may find competitiveness useful, provided that ways are found of directing competitiveness into channels that serve the needs of the system. We can imagine a future society in which there is endless competition for positions of prestige and power. But no more than a very few people will ever reach the top, where the only real power is (see end of paragraph 163). Very repellent is a society in which a person can satisfy his need for power only by pushing large numbers of other people out of the way and depriving them of *their* opportunity for power.

176. One can envision scenarios that incorporate aspects of more than one of the possibilities that we have just discussed. For instance, it may be that machines will take over most of the work that is of real, practical importance, but that human beings will be kept busy by being given relatively unimportant work. It has been suggested, for example, that a great development of the service industries might provide work for human beings. Thus

people would spend their time shining each other's shoes, driving each other around in taxicabs, making handicrafts for one another, waiting on each other's tables, etc. This seems to us a thoroughly contemptible way for the human race to end up, and we doubt that many people would find fulfilling lives in such pointless busy-work. They would seek other, dangerous outlets (drugs, crime, "cults," hate groups) unless they were biologically or psychologically engineered to adapt them to such a way of life.

177. Needless to say, the scenarios outlined above do not exhaust all the possibilities. They only indicate the kinds of outcomes that seem to us most likely. But we can envision no plausible scenarios that are any more palatable than the ones we've just described. It is overwhelmingly probable that if the industrial-technological system survives the next forty to one hundred years, it will by that time have developed certain general characteristics: Individuals (at least those of the "bourgeois" type, who are integrated into the system and make it run, and who therefore have all the power) will be more dependent than ever on large organizations; they will be more "socialized" than ever and their physical and mental qualities to a significant extent (possibly to a very great extent) will be those that are engineered into them rather than being the results of chance (or of God's will, or whatever); and whatever may be left of wild nature will be reduced to remnants preserved for scientific study and kept under the supervision and management of scientists (hence it will no longer be truly wild). In the long run (say a few centuries from now) it is likely that neither the human race nor any other important organisms will exist as we know them today, because once you start modifying organisms through genetic engineering there is no reason to stop at any particular point, so that the modifications will probably continue until man and other organisms have been utterly transformed.

178. Whatever else may be the case, it is certain that technology is creating for human beings a new physical and social environment radically different from the spectrum of environments to which natural selection has adapted the human race physically and psychologically. If man is not adjusted to this new environment by being artificially re-engineered, then he will be adapted to it through a long and painful process of natural selection. The former is far more likely than the latter.

179. It would be better to dump the whole stinking system and take the consequences.

60

Strategy

180. The technophiles are taking us all on an utterly reckless ride into the unknown. Many people understand something of what technological progress is doing to us, yet take a passive attitude toward it because they think it is inevitable. But we don't think it is inevitable. We think it can be stopped, and we will give here some indications of how to go about stopping it.

181. As we stated in paragraph 166, the two main tasks for the present are to promote social stress and instability in industrial society and to develop and propagate an ideology that opposes technology and the industrial system. When the system becomes sufficiently stressed and unstable, a revolution against technology may be possible. The pattern would be similar to that of the French and Russian Revolutions. French society and Russian society, for several decades prior to their respective revolutions, showed increasing signs of stress and weakness. Meanwhile, ideologies were being developed that offered a new world-view that was quite different from the old one. In the Russian case, revolutionaries were actively working to undermine the old order. Then, when the old system was put under sufficient additional stress (by financial crisis in France, by military defeat in Russia) it was swept away by revolution. What we propose is something along the same lines.

182. It will be objected that the French and Russian Revolutions were failures. But most revolutions have two goals. One is to destroy an old form of society and the other is to set up the new form of society envisioned by the revolutionaries. The French and Russian revolutionaries failed (fortunately!) to create the new kind of society of which they dreamed, but they were quite successful in destroying the old society. We have no illusions about the feasibility of creating a new, ideal form of society. Our goal is only to destroy the existing form of society.

183. But an ideology, in order to gain enthusiastic support, must have a positive ideal as well as a negative one; it must be *for* something as well as *against* something. The positive ideal that we propose is Nature. That is, *wild* nature: those aspects of the functioning of the Earth and its living things that are independent of human management and free of human interference and control. And with wild nature we include human nature, by which we mean those aspects of the functioning of the human individual that are not subject to regulation by organized society but are

products of chance, or free will, or God (depending on your religious or philosophical opinions).

184. Nature makes a perfect counter-ideal to technology for several reasons. Nature (that which is outside the power of the system) is the opposite of technology (which seeks to expand indefinitely the power of the system). Most people will agree that nature is beautiful; certainly it has tremendous popular appeal. The radical environmentalists *already* hold an ideology that exalts nature and opposes technology.[51] It is not necessary for the sake of nature to set up some chimerical utopia or any new kind of social order. Nature takes care of itself: It was a spontaneous creation that existed long before any human society, and for countless centuries many different kinds of human societies coexisted with nature without doing it an excessive amount of damage. Only with the Industrial Revolution did the effect of human society on nature become really devastating. To relieve the pressure on nature it is not necessary to create any special kind of social system, it is only necessary to get rid of industrial society. Granted, this will not solve all problems. Industrial society has already done tremendous damage to nature and it will take a very long time for the scars to heal. Besides, even pre-industrial societies can do significant damage to nature. Nevertheless, getting rid of industrial society will accomplish a great deal. It will relieve the worst of the pressure on nature so that the scars can begin to heal. It will remove the capacity of organized society to keep increasing its control over nature (including human nature). Whatever kind of society may exist after the demise of the industrial system, it is certain that most people will live close to nature, because in the absence of advanced technology there is no other way that people *can* live. To feed themselves they must be peasants, or herdsmen, or fishermen, or hunters, etc. And, generally speaking, local autonomy should tend to increase, because lack of advanced technology and rapid communications will limit the capacity of governments or other large organizations to control local communities.

185. As for the negative consequences of eliminating industrial society—well, you can't eat your cake and have it too. To gain one thing you have to sacrifice another.

186. Most people hate psychological conflict. For this reason they avoid doing any serious thinking about difficult social issues, and they like to have such issues presented to them in simple, black-and-white terms:

this is all good and *that* is all bad. The revolutionary ideology should therefore be developed on two levels.[52]

187. On the more sophisticated level the ideology should address itself to people who are intelligent, thoughtful and rational. The object should be to create a core of people who will be opposed to the industrial system on a rational, thought-out basis, with full appreciation of the problems and ambiguities involved, and of the price that has to be paid for getting rid of the system. It is particularly important to attract people of this type, as they are capable people and will be instrumental in influencing others. These people should be addressed on as rational a level as possible. Facts should never intentionally be distorted and intemperate language should be avoided. This does not mean that no appeal can be made to the emotions, but in making such appeal care should be taken to avoid misrepresenting the truth or doing anything else that would destroy the intellectual respectability of the ideology.

188. On a second level, the ideology should be propagated in a simplified form that will enable the unthinking majority to see the conflict of technology vs. nature in unambiguous terms. But even on this second level the ideology should not be expressed in language that is so cheap, intemperate or irrational that it alienates people of the thoughtful and rational type. Cheap, intemperate propaganda sometimes achieves impressive short-term gains, but it will be more advantageous in the long run to keep the loyalty of a small number of intelligently committed people than to arouse the passions of an unthinking, fickle mob who will change their attitude as soon as someone comes along with a better propaganda gimmick. However, propaganda of the rabble-rousing type may be necessary when the system is nearing the point of collapse and there is a final struggle between rival ideologies to determine which will become dominant when the old world-view goes under.

189. Prior to that final struggle, the revolutionaries should not expect to have a majority of people on their side. History is made by active, determined minorities, not by the majority, which seldom has a clear and consistent idea of what it really wants. Until the time comes for the final push toward revolution,[53] the task of revolutionaries will be less to win the shallow support of the majority than to build a small core of deeply committed people. As for the majority, it will be enough to make them aware of the existence of the new ideology and remind them of it frequently; though

of course it will be desirable to get majority support to the extent that this can be done without weakening the core of seriously committed people.

190. Any kind of social conflict helps to destabilize the system, but one should be careful about what kind of conflict one encourages. The line of conflict should be drawn between the mass of the people and the power-holding elite of industrial society (politicians, scientists, upper-level business executives, government officials, etc.). It should *not* be drawn between the revolutionaries and the mass of the people. For example, it would be bad strategy for the revolutionaries to condemn Americans for their habits of consumption. Instead, the average American should be portrayed as a victim of the advertising and marketing industry, which has suckered him into buying a lot of junk that he doesn't need and that is very poor compensation for his lost freedom. Either approach is consistent with the facts. It is merely a matter of attitude whether you blame the advertising industry for manipulating the public or blame the public for allowing itself to be manipulated. As a matter of strategy one should generally avoid blaming the public.

191. One should think twice before encouraging any other social conflict than that between the power-holding elite (which wields technology) and the general public (over which technology exerts its power). For one thing, other conflicts tend to distract attention from the important conflicts (between power-elite and ordinary people, between technology and nature); for another thing, other conflicts may actually tend to encourage technologization, because each side in such a conflict wants to use technological power to gain advantages over its adversary. This is clearly seen in rivalries between nations. It also appears in ethnic conflicts within nations. For example, in America many black leaders are anxious to gain power for African-Americans by placing black individuals in the technological power-elite. They want there to be many black government officials, scientists, corporation executives and so forth. In this way they are helping to absorb the African-American subculture into the technological system. Generally speaking, one should encourage only those social conflicts that can be fitted into the framework of the conflicts of power-elite vs. ordinary people, technology vs. nature.

192. But the way to discourage ethnic conflict is *not* through militant advocacy of minority rights (see paragraphs 21, 29). Instead, the revolutionaries should emphasize that although minorities do suffer more or

less disadvantage, this disadvantage is of peripheral significance. Our real enemy is the industrial-technological system, and in the struggle against the system, ethnic distinctions are of no importance.

193. The kind of revolution we have in mind will not necessarily involve an armed uprising against any government. It may or may not involve physical violence, but it will not be a *political* revolution. Its focus will be on technology and economics, not politics.

194. Probably the revolutionaries should even *avoid* assuming political power, whether by legal or illegal means, until the industrial system is stressed to the danger point and has proven itself to be a failure in the eyes of most people. Suppose for example that some "green" party should win control of the United States Congress in an election. In order to avoid betraying or watering down their own ideology they would have to take vigorous measures to turn economic growth into economic shrinkage. To the average man the results would appear disastrous: There would be massive unemployment, shortages of commodities, etc. Even if the grosser ill effects could be avoided through superhumanly skillful management, still people would have to begin giving up the luxuries to which they have become addicted. Dissatisfaction would grow, the "green" party would be voted out of office and the revolutionaries would have suffered a severe setback. For this reason the revolutionaries should not try to acquire political power until the system has gotten itself into such a mess that any hardships will be seen as resulting from the failures of the industrial system itself and not from the policies of the revolutionaries. The revolution against technology will probably have to be a revolution by outsiders, a revolution from below and not from above.

195. The revolution must be international and worldwide. It cannot be carried out on a nation-by-nation basis. Whenever it is suggested that the United States, for example, should cut back on technological progress or economic growth, people get hysterical and start screaming that if we fall behind in technology the Japanese will get ahead of us. Holy robots! The world will fly off its orbit if the Japanese ever sell more cars than we do! (Nationalism is a great promoter of technology.) More reasonably, it is argued that if the relatively democratic nations of the world fall behind in technology while nasty, dictatorial nations like China, Vietnam and North Korea continue to progress, eventually the dictators may come to dominate the world. That is why the industrial system should be attacked in all

nations simultaneously, to the extent that this may be possible. True, there is no assurance that the industrial system can be destroyed at approximately the same time all over the world, and it is even conceivable that the attempt to overthrow the system could lead instead to the domination of the system by dictators. That is a risk that has to be taken. And it is worth taking, since the difference between a "democratic" industrial system and one controlled by dictators is small compared with the difference between an industrial system and a non-industrial one.[54] It might even be argued that an industrial system controlled by dictators would be preferable, because dictator-controlled systems usually have proven inefficient, hence they are presumably more likely to break down. Look at Cuba.

196. Revolutionaries might consider favoring measures that tend to bind the world economy into a unified whole. Free trade agreements like NAFTA (North American Free Trade Agreement) and GATT (General Agreement on Tariffs and Trade) are probably harmful to the environment in the short run, but in the long run they may perhaps be advantageous because they foster economic interdependence between nations. It will be easier to destroy the industrial system on a worldwide basis if the world economy is so unified that its breakdown in any one major nation will lead to its breakdown in all industrialized nations.

197. Some people take the line that modern man has too much power, too much control over nature; they argue for a more passive attitude on the part of the human race. At best these people are expressing themselves unclearly, because they fail to distinguish between power for *large organizations* and power for *individuals* and *small groups*. It is a mistake to argue for powerlessness and passivity, because people *need* power. Modern man as a collective entity—that is, the industrial system—has immense power over nature, and we (FC) regard this as evil. But modern *individuals* and *small groups of individuals* have far less power than primitive man ever did. Generally speaking, the vast power of "modern man" over nature is exercised not by individuals or small groups but by large organizations. To the extent that the average modern *individual* can wield the power of technology, he is permitted to do so only within narrow limits and only under the supervision and control of the system. (You need a license for everything and with the license come rules and regulations.) The individual has only those technological powers with which the system chooses to provide him. His *personal* power over nature is slight.

198. Primitive *individuals* and *small groups* actually had considerable power over nature; or maybe it would be better to say power *within* nature. When primitive man needed food he knew how to find and prepare edible roots, how to track game and take it with homemade weapons. He knew how to protect himself from heat, cold, rain, dangerous animals, etc. But primitive man did relatively little damage to nature because the *collective* power of primitive society was negligible compared to the *collective* power of industrial society.

199. Instead of arguing for powerlessness and passivity, one should argue that the power of the *industrial system* should be broken, and that this will greatly *increase* the power and freedom of *individuals* and s*mall groups*.

200. Until the industrial system has been thoroughly wrecked, the destruction of that system must be the revolutionaries' *only* goal. Other goals would distract attention and energy from the main goal. More importantly, if the revolutionaries permit themselves to have any other goal than the destruction of technology, they will be tempted to use technology as a tool for reaching that other goal. If they give in to that temptation, they will fall right back into the technological trap, because modern technology is a unified, tightly organized system, so that, in order to retain *some* technology, one finds oneself obliged to retain *most* technology, hence one ends up sacrificing only token amounts of technology.

201. Suppose for example that the revolutionaries took "social justice" as a goal. Human nature being what it is, social justice would not come about spontaneously; it would have to be enforced. In order to enforce it the revolutionaries would have to retain central organization and control. For that they would need rapid long-distance transportation and communication, and therefore all the technology needed to support the transportation and communication systems. To feed and clothe poor people they would have to use agricultural and manufacturing technology. And so forth. So that the attempt to ensure social justice would force them to retain most parts of the technological system. Not that we have anything against social justice, but it must not be allowed to interfere with the effort to get rid of the technological system.

202. It would be hopeless for revolutionaries to try to attack the system without using *some* modern technology. If nothing else they must use the communications media to spread their message. But they should use

modern technology for only *one* purpose: to attack the technological system.

203. Imagine an alcoholic sitting with a barrel of wine in front of him. Suppose he starts saying to himself, "Wine isn't bad for you if used in moderation. Why, they say small amounts of wine are even good for you! It won't do me any harm if I take just one little drink... ." Well, you know what is going to happen. Never forget that the human race with technology is just like an alcoholic with a barrel of wine.

204. Revolutionaries should have as many children as they can.[55] There is strong scientific evidence that social attitudes are to a significant extent inherited. No one suggests that a social attitude is a direct outcome of a person's genetic constitution, but it appears that personality traits are partly inherited and that certain personality traits tend, within the context of our society, to make a person more likely to hold this or that social attitude. Objections to these findings have been raised, but the objections are feeble and seem to be ideologically motivated. In any event, no one denies that children tend on the average to hold social attitudes similar to those of their parents. From our point of view it doesn't matter much whether the attitudes are passed on genetically or through childhood training. In either case they *are* passed on.

205. The trouble is that many of the people who are inclined to rebel against the industrial system are also concerned about the population problem, hence they are apt to have few or no children. In this way they may be handing the world over to the sort of people who support or at least accept the industrial system. To ensure the strength of the next generation of revolutionaries the present generation should reproduce itself abundantly. In doing so they will be worsening the population problem only slightly. And the most important problem is to get rid of the industrial system, because once the industrial system is gone the world's population necessarily will decrease (see paragraph 167); whereas, if the industrial system survives, it will continue developing new techniques of food production that may enable the world's population to keep increasing almost indefinitely.

206. With regard to revolutionary strategy, the only points on which we absolutely insist are that the single, overriding goal must be the elimination of modern technology, and that no other goal can be allowed to compete with this one. For the rest, revolutionaries should take an empirical approach. If experience indicates that some of the recommendations

made in the foregoing paragraphs are not going to give good results, then those recommendations should be discarded.

Two Kinds of Technology

207. An argument likely to be raised against our proposed revolution is that it is bound to fail, because (it is claimed) throughout history technology has always progressed, never regressed, hence technological regression is impossible. But this claim is false.

208. We distinguish between two kinds of technology, which we will call *small-scale technology* and *organization-dependent technology*. Small-scale technology is technology that can be used by small-scale communities without outside assistance. Organization-dependent technology is technology that depends on large-scale social organization. We are aware of no significant cases of regression in small-scale technology.[56] But organization-dependent technology *does* regress when the social organization on which it depends breaks down. Example: When the Roman Empire fell apart the Romans' small-scale technology survived because any clever village craftsman could build, for instance, a water wheel, any skilled smith could make steel by Roman methods, and so forth. But the Romans' organization-dependent technology *did* regress. Their aqueducts fell into disrepair and were never rebuilt. Their techniques of road construction were lost. The Roman system of urban sanitation was forgotten, so that not until rather recent times did the sanitation of European cities equal that of ancient Rome.[57]

209. The reason why technology has seemed always to progress is that, until perhaps a century or two before the Industrial Revolution, most technology was small-scale technology. But most of the technology developed since the Industrial Revolution is organization-dependent technology. Take the refrigerator, for example. Without factory-made parts or the facilities of a modern machine shop, it would be virtually impossible for a handful of local craftsmen to build a refrigerator. If by some miracle they did succeed in building one it would be useless to them without a reliable source of electric power. So they would have to dam a stream and build a generator. Generators require large amounts of copper wire. Imagine trying to make that wire without modern machinery. And where would they get a gas suitable for refrigeration? It would be much easier to build an icehouse or preserve food by drying or pickling, as was done before the in-

vention of the refrigerator.

210. So it is clear that if the industrial system were once thoroughly broken down, refrigeration technology would quickly be lost. The same is true of other organization-dependent technology. And once this technology had been lost for a generation or so it would take centuries to rebuild it, just as it took centuries to build it the first time around. Surviving technical books would be few and scattered. An industrial society, if built from scratch without outside help, can only be built in a series of stages: You need tools to make tools to make tools to make tools ... . A long process of economic development and progress in social organization is required. And, even in the absence of an ideology opposed to technology, there is no reason to believe that anyone would be interested in rebuilding industrial society. The enthusiasm for "progress" is a phenomenon peculiar to the modern form of society, and it seems not to have existed prior to the 17th century or thereabouts.[58]

211. In the late Middle Ages there were four main civilizations that were about equally "advanced": Europe, the Islamic world, India, and the Far East (China, Japan, Korea). Three of those civilizations remained more or less stable, and only Europe became dynamic. No one knows why Europe became dynamic at that time; historians have their theories, but these are only speculation. At any rate, it is clear that rapid development toward a technological form of society occurs only under special conditions. So there is no reason to assume that a long-lasting technological regression cannot be brought about.

212. Would society *eventually* develop again toward an industrial-technological form? Maybe, but there is no use in worrying about it, since we can't predict or control events five hundred or a thousand years in the future. Those problems will have to be dealt with by the people who will live at that time.

The Danger of Leftism

213. Because of their need for rebellion and for membership in a movement, leftists or persons of similar psychological type often are attracted to a rebellious or activist movement whose goals and membership are not initially leftist. The resulting influx of leftish types can easily turn a non-leftist movement into a leftist one, so that leftist goals replace or distort the original goals of the movement.

214. To avoid this, a movement that exalts nature and opposes technology must take a resolutely anti-leftist stance and must avoid all collaboration with leftists. Leftism is in the long run inconsistent with wild nature, with human freedom and with the elimination of modern technology. Leftism is collectivist; it seeks to bind together the entire world (both nature and the human race) into a unified whole. But this implies management of nature and of human life by organized society, and it requires advanced technology. You can't have a united world without rapid long-distance transportation and communication, you can't make all people love one another without sophisticated psychological techniques, you can't have a "planned society" without the necessary technological base. Above all, leftism is driven by the need for power, and the leftist seeks power on a collective basis, through identification with a mass movement or an organization. Leftism is unlikely ever to give up technology, because technology is too valuable a source of collective power.

215. The anarchist[59] too seeks power, but he seeks it on an individual or small-group basis; he wants individuals and small groups to be able to control the circumstances of their own lives. He opposes technology because it makes small groups dependent on large organizations.

216. Some leftists may seem to oppose technology, but they will oppose it only as long as they are outsiders and the technological system is controlled by non-leftists. If leftism ever becomes dominant in society, so that the technological system becomes a tool in the hands of leftists, they will enthusiastically use it and promote its growth. In doing this they will be repeating a pattern that leftism has shown again and again in the past. When the Bolsheviks in Russia were outsiders, they vigorously opposed censorship and the secret police, they advocated self-determination for ethnic minorities, and so forth; but as soon as they came into power themselves, they imposed a tighter censorship and created a more ruthless secret police than any that had existed under the tsars, and they oppressed ethnic minorities at least as much as the tsars had done. In the United States, during the 1960s when leftists were a minority in our universities, leftist professors were vigorous proponents of academic freedom, but today, in those of our universities where leftists have become dominant, they have shown themselves ready to take away everyone else's academic freedom. (This is "political correctness.") The same will happen with leftists and technology: They will use it to oppress everyone else if they ever get it under their own control.

217. In earlier revolutions, leftists of the most power-hungry type, repeatedly, have first cooperated with non-leftist revolutionaries, as well as with leftists of a more libertarian inclination, and later have double-crossed them to seize power for themselves. Robespierre did this in the French Revolution, the Bolsheviks did it in the Russian Revolution, the communists did it in Spain in 1938, and Castro and his followers did it in Cuba. Given the past history of leftism, it would be utterly foolish for non-leftist revolutionaries today to collaborate with leftists.

218. Various thinkers have pointed out that leftism is a kind of religion. Leftism is not a religion in the strict sense, because leftist doctrine does not postulate the existence of any supernatural being. But, for the leftist, leftism plays a psychological role much like that which religion plays for some people. The leftist *needs* to believe in leftism; it plays a vital role in his psychological economy. His beliefs are not easily modified by logic or facts. He has a deep conviction that leftism is morally Right with a capital R, and that he has not only a right but a duty to impose leftist morality on everyone. (However, many of the people we are referring to as "leftists" do not think of themselves as leftists and would not describe their system of beliefs as leftism. We use the term "leftism" because we don't know of any better word to designate the spectrum of related creeds that includes the feminist, gay rights, political correctness, etc., movements, and because these movements have a strong affinity with the old left. See paragraphs 227–230.)

219. Leftism is a totalitarian force. Wherever leftism is in a position of power it tends to invade every private corner and force every thought into a leftist mold. In part this is because of the quasi-religious character of leftism; everything contrary to leftist beliefs represents Sin. More importantly, leftism is a totalitarian force because of the leftists' drive for power. The leftist seeks to satisfy his need for power through identification with a social movement, and he tries to go through the power process by helping to pursue and attain the goals of the movement (see paragraph 83). But no matter how far the movement has gone in attaining its goals the leftist is never satisfied, because his activism is a surrogate activity (see paragraph 41). That is, the leftist's real motive is not to attain the ostensible goals of leftism; in reality he is motivated by the sense of power he gets from struggling for and then reaching a social goal.[60] Consequently, the leftist is never satisfied with the goals he has already attained; his need for

the power process leads him always to pursue some new goal. The leftist wants equal opportunities for minorities. When that is attained he insists on statistical equality of achievement by minorities. And as long as anyone harbors in some corner of his mind a negative attitude toward some minority, the leftist has to re-educate him. And ethnic minorities are not enough; no one can be allowed to have a negative attitude toward homosexuals, disabled people, fat people, old people, ugly people, and on and on and on. It's not enough that the public should be informed about the hazards of smoking; a warning has to be stamped on every package of cigarettes. Then cigarette advertising has to be restricted if not banned. The activists will never be satisfied until tobacco is outlawed, and after that it will be alcohol, then junk food, etc. Activists have fought gross child abuse, which is reasonable. But now they want to stop all spanking. When they have done that they will want to ban something else they consider unwholesome, then another thing and then another. They will never be satisfied until they have complete control over all child-rearing practices. And then they will move on to another cause.

220. Suppose you asked leftists to make a list of *all* the things that were wrong with society, and then suppose you instituted *every* social change that they demanded. It is safe to say that within a couple of years the majority of leftists would find something new to complain about, some new social "evil" to correct, because, once again, the leftist is motivated less by distress at society's ills than by the need to satisfy his drive for power by imposing his solutions on society.

221. Because of the restrictions placed on their thought and behavior by their high level of socialization, many leftists of the oversocialized type cannot pursue power in the ways that other people do. For them the drive for power has only one morally acceptable outlet, and that is in the struggle to impose their morality on everyone.

222. Leftists, especially those of the oversocialized type, are True Believers in the sense of Eric Hoffer's book, *The True Believer*. But not all True Believers are of the same psychological type as leftists. Presumably a true-believing Nazi, for instance, is very different psychologically from a true-believing leftist.[61] Because of their capacity for single-minded devotion to a cause, True Believers are a useful, perhaps a necessary, ingredient of any revolutionary movement. This presents a problem with which we must admit we don't know how to deal. We aren't sure how to harness the

energies of the True Believer to a revolution against technology. At present all we can say is that no True Believer will make a safe recruit to the revolution unless his commitment is exclusively to the destruction of technology. If he is committed also to another ideal, he may want to use technology as a tool for pursuing that other ideal. (See paragraphs 200, 201.)

223. Some readers may say, "This stuff about leftism is a lot of crap. I know John and Jane who are leftish types, and they don't have all these totalitarian tendencies." It's quite true that many leftists, possibly even a numerical majority, are decent people who sincerely believe in tolerating others' values (up to a point) and wouldn't want to use high-handed methods to reach their social goals. Our remarks about leftism are not meant to apply to every individual leftist, but to describe the general character of leftism as a movement. And the general character of a movement is not necessarily determined by the numerical proportions of the various kinds of people involved in the movement.

224. The people who rise to positions of power in leftist movements tend to be leftists of the most power-hungry type,[62] because power-hungry people are those who strive hardest to get into positions of power. Once the power-hungry types have captured control of the movement, there are many leftists of a gentler breed who inwardly disapprove of many of the actions of the leaders, but cannot bring themselves to oppose them. They *need* their faith in the movement, and because they cannot give up this faith they go along with the leaders. True, *some* leftists do have the guts to oppose the totalitarian tendencies that emerge, but they generally lose, because the power-hungry types are better organized, are more ruthless and Machiavellian, and have taken care to build themselves a strong power-base.

225. These phenomena appeared clearly in Russia and other countries that were taken over by leftists. Similarly, before the breakdown of communism in the USSR, leftish types in the West would seldom criticize that country. If prodded they would admit that the USSR did many wrong things, but then they would try to find excuses for the communists and begin talking about the faults of the West. They always opposed Western military resistance to communist aggression. Leftish types all over the world vigorously protested the U.S. military action in Vietnam, but when the USSR invaded Afghanistan they did nothing. Not that they approved of the Soviet actions; but because of their leftist faith, they just

couldn't bear to put themselves in opposition to communism. Today, in those of our universities where "political correctness" has become dominant, there are probably many leftish types who privately disapprove of the suppression of academic freedom, but they go along with it anyway.

226. Thus, the fact that many individual leftists are personally mild and fairly tolerant people by no means prevents leftism as a whole from having a totalitarian tendency.

227. Our discussion of leftism has a serious weakness. It is still far from clear what we mean by the word "leftist." There doesn't seem to be much we can do about this. Leftism today is fragmented into a whole spectrum of activist movements. Yet not all activist movements are leftist, and some activist movements (e.g., radical environmentalism) seem to include both personalities of the leftist type and personalities of thoroughly un-leftist types who ought to know better than to collaborate with leftists. Varieties of leftists fade out gradually into varieties of non-leftists, and we ourselves would often be hard-pressed to decide whether a given individual is or is not a leftist. To the extent that it is defined at all, our conception of leftism is defined by the discussion of it that we have given in this article, and we can only advise the reader to use his own judgment in deciding who is a leftist.

228. But it will be helpful to list some criteria for diagnosing leftism. These criteria cannot be applied in a cut and dried manner. Some individuals may meet some of the criteria without being leftists, some leftists may not meet any of the criteria. Again, you just have to use your judgment.

229. The leftist is oriented toward large-scale collectivism. He emphasizes the duty of the individual to serve society and the duty of society to take care of the individual. He has a negative attitude toward individualism. He often takes a moralistic tone. He tends to be for gun control, for sex education and other psychologically "enlightened" educational methods, for social planning, for affirmative action, for multiculturalism. He tends to identify with victims. He tends to be against competition and against violence, but he often finds excuses for those leftists who do commit violence. He is fond of using the common catch-phrases of the left, like "racism," "sexism," "homophobia," "capitalism," "imperialism," "neocolonialism," "genocide," "social change," "social justice," "social responsibility." Maybe the best diagnostic trait of the leftist is his tendency to sympathize with the following movements: feminism, gay rights, ethnic rights, disabil-

ity rights, animal rights, political correctness. Anyone who strongly sympathizes with *all* of these movements is almost certainly a leftist.[63]

230. The more dangerous leftists, that is, those who are most power-hungry, are often characterized by arrogance or by a dogmatic approach to ideology. However, the most dangerous leftists of all may be certain oversocialized types who avoid irritating displays of aggressiveness and refrain from advertising their leftism, but work quietly and unobtrusively to promote collectivist values, "enlightened" psychological techniques for socializing children, dependence of the individual on the system, and so forth. These crypto-leftists (as we may call them) approximate certain bourgeois types as far as practical action is concerned, but differ from them in psychology, ideology and motivation. The ordinary bourgeois tries to bring people under control of the system in order to protect his way of life, or he does so simply because his attitudes are conventional. The crypto-leftist tries to bring people under control of the system because he is a True Believer in a collectivistic ideology. The crypto-leftist is differentiated from the average leftist of the oversocialized type by the fact that his rebellious impulse is weaker and he is more securely socialized. He is differentiated from the ordinary well-socialized bourgeois by the fact that there is some deep lack within him that makes it necessary for him to devote himself to a cause and immerse himself in a collectivity. And maybe his (well-sublimated) drive for power is stronger than that of the average bourgeois.

Final Note

231. Throughout this article we've made imprecise statements and statements that ought to have had all sorts of qualifications and reservations attached to them; and some of our statements may be flatly false. Lack of sufficient information and the need for brevity have made it impossible for us to formulate our assertions more precisely or add all the necessary qualifications. And, of course, in a discussion of this kind one must rely heavily on intuitive judgment, and that can sometimes be wrong. So we don't claim that this article expresses more than a crude approximation to the truth.

232. All the same, we are reasonably confident that the general outlines of the picture we have painted here are roughly correct. Just one possible weak point needs to be mentioned. We have portrayed leftism in its

modern form as a phenomenon peculiar to our time and as a symptom of the disruption of the power process. But we might possibly be wrong about this. Oversocialized types who try to satisfy their drive for power by imposing their morality on everyone have certainly been around for a long time. But we *think* that the decisive role played by feelings of inferiority, low self-esteem, powerlessness, identification with victims by people who are not themselves victims, is a peculiarity of modern leftism. Identification with victims by people not themselves victims can be seen to some extent in 19th-century leftism and early Christianity, but as far as we can make out, symptoms of low self-esteem, etc., were not nearly so evident in these movements, or in any other movements, as they are in modern leftism. But we are not in a position to assert confidently that no such movements have existed prior to modern leftism. This is a significant question to which historians ought to give their attention.

NOTES

1. (¶ 1) (Added 2016) See in *Technological Slavery, Volume One*: Letter to Dr. Skrbina of Nov. 23, 2004, Part III.E.

2. (¶ 19) We are not asserting that all, or even most, bullies and ruthless competitors suffer from feelings of inferiority.

3. (¶ 25) During the Victorian period many oversocialized people suffered from serious psychological problems as a result of repressing or trying to repress their sexual feelings. Freud apparently based his theories on people of this type. Today the focus of socialization has shifted from sex to aggression.

4. (¶ 27) Not necessarily including specialists in engineering or the "hard" sciences.

5. (¶ 28) There are many individuals of the middle and upper classes who resist some of these values, but usually their resistance is more or less covert. Such resistance appears in the mass media only to a very limited extent. The main thrust of propaganda in our society is in favor of the stated values. The principal reason why these values have become, so to speak, the official values of our society is that they are useful to the industrial system. Violence is discouraged because it disrupts the functioning of the system. Racism is discouraged because ethnic conflicts also disrupt the system, and discrimination wastes the talents of minority-group members who could be useful to the system. Poverty must be "cured" because the underclass causes problems for the system and contact with the underclass lowers the morale of the other classes. Women are encouraged to have careers because their talents are useful to the system and, more importantly, because by having regular jobs women become integrated into the system and tied

directly to it rather than to their families. This helps to weaken family solidarity. (The leaders of the system say they want to strengthen the family, but what they really mean is that they want the family to serve as an effective tool for socializing children in accord with the needs of the system. We argue in paragraphs 51, 52 that the system cannot afford to let the family or other small-scale social groups be strong or autonomous.)

6. (¶¶ 33-37) (Added 2016) See in *Technological Slavery, Volume One*: Letter to Dr. Skrbina of Oct. 12, 2004, Part I; and Appendix One.

7. (¶ 42) It may be argued that the majority of people don't want to make their own decisions, but want leaders to do their thinking for them. There is an element of truth in this. People like to make their own decisions in small matters, but making decisions on difficult, fundamental questions requires facing up to psychological conflict, and most people hate psychological conflict. Hence they tend to lean on others in making difficult decisions. But it does not follow that they like to have decisions imposed on them without having any opportunity to influence those decisions. The majority of people are natural followers, not leaders, but they like to have direct personal access to their leaders, they want to be able to influence the leaders and participate to some extent in making even the difficult decisions. At least to that degree they need autonomy.

8. (¶ 44) (Supplemented 2016) Some of the symptoms listed are similar to those shown by caged animals. See Morris, passim, especially pp. 160–225. To explain how these symptoms arise from deprivation with respect to the power process: Common-sense understanding of human nature tells one that lack of goals whose attainment requires effort leads to boredom and that boredom, long continued, often leads eventually to depression. Failure to attain goals leads to frustration and lowering of self-esteem. Frustration leads to anger, anger to aggression, often in the form of spouse or child abuse. It has been shown that long-continued frustration commonly leads to depression and that depression tends to cause anxiety, guilt, sleep disorders, eating disorders, and bad feelings about oneself. Those who are tending toward depression seek pleasure as an antidote; hence insatiable hedonism and excessive sex, with perversions as a means of getting new kicks. Boredom too tends to cause excessive pleasure-seeking since, lacking other goals, people often use pleasure as a goal. The foregoing is a simplification. Reality is more complex, and of course deprivation with respect to the power process is not the *only* cause of the symptoms described. By the way, when we mention depression we do not necessarily mean depression that is severe enough to be treated by a psychiatrist. Often only mild forms of depression are involved. And when we speak of goals we do not necessarily mean long-term, thought-out goals. For many or most people through much of human history, the goals of a hand-to-mouth existence (merely providing oneself and one's family

with food and other necessities from day to day) have been quite sufficient.

9. (¶ 52) (Modified 2016) A partial exception may be made for a few passive, inward-looking groups, such as the Amish, which have little effect on the wider society. Apart from these, some genuine small-scale communities do exist in America today. For instance, youth gangs and "cults." Everyone regards them as dangerous, and so they are, because the members of these groups are loyal primarily to one another rather than to the system, hence the system cannot control them. Or take the gypsies. The gypsies commonly get away with theft and fraud because their loyalties are such that they can always get other gypsies to give testimony that "proves" their innocence. See, e.g., Maas, pp. 78–79. Obviously the system would be in serious trouble if too many people belonged to such groups. For some relevant examples, see Appendix Six of *Technological Slavery, Volume One*. Also see Carrillo, pp. 46–47.

10. (¶ 54) (Added 2016) Actually, it's open to question whether the problems tend to be less acute in rural areas. Compare *The Week*, Oct. 17, 2008, p. 14, "The myth of small-town superiority" with *The Economist*, June 25, 2011, p. 94, "A New York state of mind." The main point stands in any case: that crowding is not the decisive factor.

11. (¶ 55) (Added 2016) E.g.: "In a fashion that men and women of the twentieth century will never fully understand, farmers of the Mississippi valley and the Plains states [in the 1830s or 1840s] had begun to feel 'crowded.' One farmer said that the reason he had to emigrate from western Illinois was that 'people were settling right under his nose,' although his nearest neighbor was twelve miles away." Schlissel, p. 20, citing Bright, p. 246. See also Dick, p. 25.

12. (¶ 56) Yes, we know that 19th-century America had its problems, and serious ones, but for the sake of brevity we have to express ourselves in simplified terms.

13. (¶ 61) We leave aside the "underclass." We are speaking of the mainstream.

14. (¶ 62) Some social scientists, educators, "mental health" professionals and the like are doing their best to push the social drives into group 1 by trying to see to it that everyone has a satisfactory social life.

15. (¶ 63) Is the drive for endless material acquisition really an artificial creation of the advertising and marketing industry? Certainly there is no innate human drive for material acquisition. There have been many cultures in which people have desired little material wealth beyond what was necessary to satisfy their basic physical needs (Australian aborigines, traditional Mexican peasant culture, some African cultures). On the other hand, there have also been many pre-industrial cultures in which material acquisition has played an important role. So we can't claim that today's acquisition-oriented culture is exclusively a creation

of the advertising and marketing industry. But it is clear that the advertising and marketing industry has had an important part in creating that culture. The big corporations that spend millions on advertising wouldn't be spending that kind of money without solid proof that they were getting it back in increased sales.

(Added 2016) In searching for a summer job in 1958, I answered a classified ad that led me to an office in Chicago. From there I was taken with several other teenagers to a suburban neighborhood, where we were all turned loose to sell magazine subscriptions from door to door. None of us succeeded in selling even one. Afterward the man in charge told us frankly, "Our job is to make people buy things they don't want and don't need." He then explained that the same neighborhood would be covered later by experienced professional salesmen who would sell numerous subscriptions where we had sold none at all. Evidently the objective of our excursion had not actually been to sell subscriptions; maybe it was simply to test out the youths in question. Whatever the objective may have been, the foregoing account illustrates the fact that professionals can and do manipulate people into buying things they don't really want.

As ISAIF was originally written, the incident described here was altered to avoid any risk that the author could be identified; the present account is accurate.

16. (¶ 64) The problem of purposelessness seems to have become less serious during the last 15 years or so [this refers to the 15 years preceding 1995], because people now feel less secure physically and economically than they did earlier, and the need for security provides them with a goal. But purposelessness has been replaced by frustration over the difficulty of attaining security. We emphasize the problem of purposelessness because the liberals and leftists would wish to solve our social problems by having society guarantee everyone's security; but if that could be done it would only bring back the problem of purposelessness. The real issue is not whether society provides well or poorly for people's security; the trouble is that people are dependent on the system for their security rather than having it in their own hands. This, by the way, is part of the reason why some people get worked up about the right to bear arms; possession of a gun puts that aspect of their security in their own hands.

17. (¶ 65) (Added 2016) The following item appeared in *The Missoulian*, May 25, 1988, under the title "Small businesses, take heart": "... 'But if you're a true entrepreneur, you may not qualify for a franchise. Franchise Development Inc. of Pittsburgh says its clients have been using 2 ½-hour psychological tests to ferret out those with strong entrepreneurial qualities, such as creativity and independence—just the people who become "troublemakers" by refusing to work within the franchise system.' *Wall Street Journal*."

18. (¶ 66) Conservatives' efforts to decrease the amount of government regulation are of little benefit to the average man. For one thing, only a fraction of

the regulations can be eliminated because most regulations are necessary. For another thing, most of the deregulation affects business rather than the average individual, so that its main effect is to take power from the government and give it to private corporations. What this means for the average man is that government interference in his life is replaced by interference from big corporations, which may be permitted, for example, to dump more chemicals that get into his water supply and give him cancer. The conservatives are just taking the average man for a sucker, exploiting his resentment of Big Government to promote the power of Big Business.

19. (¶ 67) (Added 2016) Quoted by Anthony Lewis, *New York Times*, April 21, 1995.

20. (¶ 69) (Added 2016) Último Reducto has pointed out that many primitive peoples attribute sickness not to an "impersonal demon," but to witchcraft. If someone becomes seriously ill attempts are made to identify the supposed "witch," who is then killed. See, e.g., Ross, p. 154. Pre-industrial peoples believed in magic and witchcraft because such beliefs provided them with an explanation for otherwise incomprehensible negative events and with an illusion of power to ward off such events. A discussion of beliefs that serve a similar purpose in the modern world would be of considerable interest, but this is not the place for it.

21. (¶ 73) When someone approves of the purpose for which propaganda is being used in a given case, he generally calls it "education" or applies to it some similar euphemism. But propaganda is propaganda regardless of the purpose for which it is used.

22. (¶ 75) (Added 2016) I may have gone too far here. Among the Mbuti Pygmies, according to Turnbull, *Wayward Servants*, p. 127, "[The elder age group] is an age group to which a man or a woman resigns himself [sic] with some reluctance... ." It still does seem true, however, that any reluctance to grow old among primitives is far exceeded by the reluctance of many modern people, as shown by the lengths to which some of the latter will go in an effort to maintain youthfulness.

23. (¶ 83) We are not expressing approval or disapproval of the Panama invasion. We only use it to illustrate a point.

24. (¶¶ 87–92) (Added 2016) The discussion here of the motives of scientists is certainly inadequate. For a more thorough discussion, see the Letter to Dr. P.B. on the Motivations of Scientists, which appears in *Technological Slavery, Volume One*.

25. (¶ 94) (Added 2016) Último Reducto has pointed out that this definition of freedom requires refinement and/or explanation, inasmuch as people have never had full control over the circumstances of their own lives. They have not, for example, been able to control bad weather, which in some circumstances can lead to the failure of food supplies. I think the necessary refinement and explanation

of the definition can be provided, but this is not the place for it.

26. (¶ 95) When the American colonies were under British rule there were fewer and less effective legal guarantees of freedom than there were after the American Constitution went into effect, yet there was more personal freedom in pre-industrial America, both before and after the War of Independence, than there was after the Industrial Revolution took hold in this country. We quote Graham & Gurr, Chapt. 12 by Roger Lane, pp. 476–78: "The progressive heightening of standards of propriety, and with it the increasing reliance on official law enforcement [in 19th-century America]... were common to the whole society... [T]he change in social behavior is so long term and so wide-spread as to suggest a connection with the most fundamental of contemporary social processes; that of industrial urbanization itself. ...Massachusetts in 1835 had a population of some 660,940, eighty-one percent rural, overwhelmingly pre-industrial and native born. Its citizens were used to considerable personal freedom. Whether teamsters, farmers or artisans, they were all accustomed to setting their own schedules, and the nature of their work made them physically independent of each other. ...Individual problems, sins or even crimes, were not generally cause for wider social concern. ...But the impact of the twin movements to the city and to the factory, both just gathering force in 1835, had a progressive effect on personal behavior throughout the 19th century and into the 20th. The factory demanded regularity of behavior, a life governed by obedience to the rhythms of clock and calendar, the demands of foreman and supervisor. In the city or town, the needs of living in closely packed neighborhoods inhibited many actions previously unobjectionable. Both blue- and white-collar employees in larger establishments were mutually dependent on their fellows; as one man's work fit into another's, so one man's business was no longer his own. The results of the new organization of life and work were apparent by 1900, when some 76 percent of the 2,805,346 inhabitants of Massachusetts were classified as urbanites. Much violent or irregular behavior which had been tolerable in a casual, independent society was no longer acceptable in the more formalized, cooperative atmosphere of the later period. ...The move to the cities had, in short, produced a more tractable, more socialized, more 'civilized' generation than its predecessors."

27. (¶ 95) (Added 2016) Último Reducto has pointed out that the correct anthropological term here would be "chiefdoms" rather than "monarchies," but for our purposes this makes no difference.

28. (¶ 97) (Added 2016) Bolívar wrote: "No liberty is legitimate, except when aimed at the honour of mankind and the improvement of his lot." Trend, p. 114. See Appendix Six of *Technological Slavery, Volume One.*

29. (¶ 97) (Added 2016) Tan, p. 202.

30. (¶ 97) (Added 2016) Ibid., p. 259.

31. (¶ 114) See Note 21.

32. (¶ 115) (Added 2016) "The whining schoolboy, with his satchel and shining morning face, creeps like a snail unwillingly to school." Shakespeare, *As You Like It,* Act 2, Scene 7 (here slightly altered).

33. (¶ 117) Apologists for the system are fond of citing cases in which elections have been decided by one or two votes, but such cases are rare.

34. (¶ 119) "Today, in technologically advanced lands, men live very similar lives in spite of geographical, religious, and political differences. The daily lives of a Christian bank clerk in Chicago, a Buddhist bank clerk in Tokyo, and a Communist bank clerk in Moscow are far more alike than the life of any one of them is like that of any single man who lived a thousand years ago. These similarities are the result of a common technology... ." De Camp, p. 17. The lives of the three bank clerks are not *identical.* Ideology does have *some* effect. But all technological societies, in order to survive, must evolve along *approximately* the same trajectory.

35. (¶ 122) For a further example of undesirable consequences of medical progress, suppose a reliable cure for cancer is discovered. Even if the treatment is too expensive to be available to any but the elite, it will greatly reduce their incentive to stop the escape of carcinogens into the environment.

36. (¶ 123) Just think, an irresponsible genetic engineer might create a lot of terrorists.

37. (¶ 128) Since many people may find paradoxical the notion that a large number of good things can add up to a bad thing, we illustrate with an analogy. Suppose Mr. A is playing chess with Mr. B. Mr. C, a grand master, is looking over Mr. A's shoulder. Mr. A of course wants to win his game, so if Mr. C points out a good move for him to make, he is doing Mr. A a favor. But suppose now that Mr. C tells Mr. A how to make *all* of his moves. In each particular instance he does Mr. A a favor by showing him his best move, but by making *all* of his moves for him he spoils his game, since there is no point in Mr. A's playing the game at all if someone else makes all his moves. The situation of modern man is analogous to that of Mr. A. The system makes an individual's life easier for him in innumerable ways, but in doing so it deprives him of control over his own fate.

38. (¶ 131) See Note 21.

39. (¶ 137) Here we are considering only the conflict of values within the mainstream. For the sake of simplicity we leave out of the picture "outsider" values like the idea that wild nature is more important than human economic welfare.

40. (¶ 137) Self-interest is not necessarily *material* self-interest. It can consist in fulfillment of some psychological need, for example, by promoting one's own ideology or religion.

41. (¶ 139) A qualification: It is in the interest of the system to permit a certain prescribed degree of freedom in some areas. For example, economic freedom (with suitable limitations and restraints) has proven effective in promoting economic growth. But only planned, circumscribed, limited freedom is in the interest of the system. The individual must always be kept on a leash, even if the leash is sometimes long. (See paragraphs 94, 97.)

42. (¶ 143) We don't mean to suggest that the efficiency or the potential for survival of a society has always been inversely proportional to the amount of pressure or discomfort to which the society subjects people. That certainly is not the case. There is good reason to believe that many primitive societies subjected people to less pressure than European society did, but European society proved far more efficient than any primitive society and always won out in conflicts with such societies because of the advantages conferred by technology.

43. (¶ 147) If you think that more effective law enforcement is unequivocally good because it suppresses crime, then remember that crime as defined by the system is not necessarily what *you* would call crime. Today [this refers to 1995], smoking marijuana is a "crime," and, in some places in the U.S., so is possession of an unregistered handgun. Tomorrow, possession of *any* firearm, registered or not, may be made a crime, and the same thing may happen with disapproved methods of child-rearing, such as spanking. In some countries, expression of dissident political opinions is a crime, and there is no certainty that this will never happen in the U.S., since no constitution or political system lasts forever. If a society needs a large, powerful law-enforcement establishment, then there is something gravely wrong with that society; it must be subjecting people to severe pressures if so many refuse to follow the rules, or follow them only because forced. Many societies in the past have gotten by with little or no formal law-enforcement.

44. (¶ 147) (Added 2016, modified 2019) A psychological study has found that for most modern people, "simply being alone with their own thoughts for 15 min" is a highly aversive experience. See Wilson, Reinhard, et al. Compare this with the statements of the Eskimo mentioned by Durant, Chapt. II, p. 6, and the Indians described by Ferris, Chapt. LXI, as pacing in front of their lodges. See also Kaczynski, *Technological Slavery* (2010), p. 406.

45. (¶ 151) To be sure, past societies have had means of influencing human behavior, but these have been primitive and of low effectiveness compared with the technological means that are now being developed.

46. (¶ 152) (Supplemented 2016) However, some psychologists have publicly expressed opinions indicating their contempt for human freedom. E.g., "I believe that the day has come when we can combine sensory deprivation with drugs, hypnosis and astute manipulation of reward and punishment to gain almost absolute control over an individual's behavior. ...We should reshape our society so that

we all would be trained from birth to do what society wants us to do." James V. McConnell, quoted in an article titled "Behavior Control: Boon or Bane?," in the Chicago *Sun Times*, March 7, 1971. And the mathematician Claude Shannon was quoted in *Omni*, Aug. 1987, as saying: "I visualize a time when we will be to robots what dogs are to humans, and I'm rooting for the machines."

47. (¶ 153) See Note 21.

48. (¶ 154) This is no science fiction! After writing paragraph 154 we came across an article in *Scientific American* according to which scientists are actively developing techniques for identifying possible future criminals and for treating them by a combination of biological and psychological means. Some scientists advocate compulsory application of the treatment, which may be available in the near future. See W.W. Gibbs, as referenced in our List of Works Cited. Maybe you think this is okay because the treatment would be applied to those who might become violent criminals. But of course it won't stop there. Next, a treatment will be applied to those who might become drunk drivers (they endanger human life too), then perhaps to people who spank their children, then to environmentalists who sabotage logging equipment, eventually to anyone whose behavior is inconvenient for the system.

(Added 2016) The foregoing was written in 1995, but, as far as I know, compulsory treatments to prevent children from growing up to be criminals have not yet begun. This fact illustrates two points that I did not fully understand in 1995:

First, that invasions of our freedom and dignity tend to come from unexpected directions. An apparent threat to our freedom and dignity very often is never realized, or takes much longer to be realized than anyone has expected; the erosion of our freedom and dignity continues, but in ways that no one has foreseen. For example, in 1970 "strong" (i.e., human-like) artificial intelligence, which would have put excessive power into the hands of those who possessed it, was expected within 15 years or so. Darrach, p. 58. But it has not yet arrived. On the other hand, most people nowadays have become so absorbed in and dependent on computerized electronic media that the technology industry has acquired enormous power over them in a way that no one dreamed of in 1970.

The second point is that where methods for controlling human behavior require intelligent monitoring or treatment of individuals, they are excessively difficult to apply effectively throughout an entire population. Thus our criminal-justice system, to the extent that it operates by attempting to manipulate actual or potential offenders on an individualized basis, is expensive and ineffective as a tool for controlling the behavior of the criminal population as a whole. The same can be said of our educational system to the extent that it tries to manipulate students individually. Present-day society therefore relies primarily on methods that can be applied on a mass basis and without taking account of individual differences, such as ubiquitous electronic surveillance that intimidates potential offenders and facilitates physical coercion, or propaganda in the widest sense of the term, for which the educational system serves as an effective vehicle.

49. (¶ 167) (Added 2016) I now think a gradual breakdown is so unlikely that we need not take that possibility into consideration. See Kaczynski, *Anti-Tech Revolution*, Chapt. Two.

50. (¶¶ 171–78) (Added 2016) I've now moved well beyond the speculations put forward here. For a far more probable vision of the future, see ibid.

51. (¶ 184) A further advantage of nature as a counter-ideal to technology is that, in many people, nature inspires the kind of reverence that is associated with religion, so that nature could perhaps be idealized on a religious basis. It is true that in many societies religion has served as a support and justification for the established order, but it is also true that religion has often provided a basis for rebellion. Thus it may be useful to introduce a religious element into the rebellion against technology, the more so because Western society today has no strong religious foundation. Religion nowadays either is used as cheap and transparent support for narrow, short-sighted selfishness (some conservatives use it this way), or even is cynically exploited to make easy money (by many evangelists), or has degenerated into crude irrationalism (fundamentalist Protestant sects, "cults"), or is simply stagnant (Catholicism, mainline Protestantism). The nearest thing to a strong, widespread, dynamic religion that the West has seen in recent times has been the quasi-religion of leftism, but leftism today is fragmented and has no clear, unified, inspiring goal. Thus there is a religious vacuum in our society that could perhaps be filled by a religion focused on nature in opposition to technology. But it would be a mistake to try to concoct artificially a religion to fill this role. Such an invented religion would probably be a failure. Take the "Gaia" religion for example. Do its adherents *really* believe in it or are they just play-acting? If they are just play-acting their religion will be a flop in the end. It is probably best not to try to introduce religion into the conflict of nature vs. technology unless you *really* believe in that religion yourself and find that it arouses a deep, strong, genuine response in many other people.

52. (¶¶ 186–88) (Added 2016) Since writing these paragraphs in 1995, I've been gratified to find these two points confirmed by authors who are much better qualified than I am to deal with this subject: ISAIF's distinction between two levels of ideology corresponds roughly to Plekhanov's and Lenin's distinction between "propaganda" and "agitation." See NEB (2003), Vol. 26, "Propaganda," p. 171; Ulam, p. 34&n21; Selznick, pp. 9–10; Lenin, *What is to be Done?*, Chapt. III, Part B; pp. 101–02 in Christman. Alinsky, pp. 27–28, 78, 133–34, stresses the importance of presenting issues in black-and-white terms in the process of agitation, with all the good on one side and all the evil on the other.

53. (¶ 189) (Modified 2016) Assuming that such a final push occurs. It's conceivable though highly unlikely that the industrial system might be eliminated in a somewhat gradual or piecemeal fashion. (See paragraphs 4, 167 and Note 49.)

54. (¶ 195) The economic and technological structure of a society are far more important than its political structure in determining the way the average man lives. (See paragraphs 95, 119 and Notes 26, 34.)

55. (¶ 204) (Added 2016) I now retract this sentence. The advice to revolutionaries to have many children may possibly have had some merit in 1995, but I now believe that the final and decisive stage of the struggle against the system will have to be conducted by people who have already been born, though perhaps with some help from the first generation that follows them. The problem with having children is that potential revolutionaries who do so usually become so involved in family matters that they are of little use as revolutionaries.

56. (¶ 208) (Added 2016) Último Reducto has pointed out some examples of regression of small-scale technology in primitive societies, but even if such examples can be found in civilized societies they will not affect our argument.

57. (¶ 208) (Added 2016) See NEB (2003), Vol. 15, "Building Construction," p. 317.

58. (¶ 210) (Added 2016) See Bury, pp. 58–60, 64–65, 113.

59. (¶ 215) This statement refers to our particular brand of anarchism. A wide variety of social attitudes have been called "anarchist," and it may be that many who consider themselves anarchists would not accept our statement of paragraph 215. It should be noted, by the way, that there is a nonviolent anarchist movement whose members probably would not accept FC as anarchist and certainly would not approve of FC's violent methods.

(Added 2016) In 1995 I described FC as "anarchist" because I thought it would be advantageous to have some recognized political identity. At that time I knew very little about anarchism. Since then I've learned that anarchists, at least those of the U.S. and the U.K., are nothing but a lot of hopelessly ineffectual bunglers and dreamers, useless for any purpose. Needless to say, I now disavow any identification as an anarchist.

60. (¶ 219) Many leftists are motivated also by hostility, but the hostility probably results in part from a frustrated need for power.

61. (¶ 222) (Added 2016) This statement will perhaps be disputed. See Hoffer, § 14. Also, Rothfels, p. 63, notes that after Hitler's seizure of power in 1933 many Communists defected to become Nazis, and vice versa after 1945 in the Soviet zone of occupied Germany. But those who switched from one party to the other under such circumstances were not necessarily True Believers. More likely they were opportunists who joined whatever party seemed to be on the winning side at any given time. Be that as it may, even if true-believing Nazis and

Communists of the first half of the 20th century were of identical psychological type, and even if one grants that all True Believers have *some* psychological traits in common, this writer finds it implausible to suppose that there are no major psychological differences between the typical Nazi and the typical true-believing leftist of recent decades in North America and Western Europe.

62. (¶ 224) (Added 2016) My use of the term "power-hungry" has caused some confusion inasmuch as I've stressed the fact that everyone needs power, hence, many readers assume that everyone should be considered power-hungry. However, the term "power-hungry" is conventionally applied only to those who seek power over other people, as in the form of political or financial power, or any power to command. Those who seek power in the form, for example, of intellectual, artistic, or athletic prowess, or manual skills, or, say, the skills needed to live independently of the technological system, are not necessarily power-hungry in the usual sense of the term.

63. (¶ 229) It is important to understand that we mean someone who sympathizes with these movements as they exist today in our society. One who believes that women, homosexuals, etc., should have equal rights is not necessarily a leftist. The feminist, gay rights, etc., movements that exist in our society have the particular ideological tone that characterizes leftism, and if one believes, for example, that women should have equal rights it does not necessarily follow that one must sympathize with the feminist movement as it exists today.

FURTHER COMMENTS (ADDED 2020)

In reference to paragraph 11, "broad," "chick," etc. In answer to this, a correspondent remarked that he would be offended if he were referred to or addressed as "dude," so some clarification is required. In many contexts, "dude" can be offensive *to the individual so addressed,* and even prior to the advent of leftist hypersensitivity "broad" or "chick" could be offensive *to the individual to whom those terms were applied.* The difference is that leftists now interpret the terms "broad" and "chick" as insulting to the entire female sex, even when those terms are applied only to particular individuals. No one feels that the entire male sex is insulted when a particular individual is called "dude."

In reference to paragraph 20, "Self-hatred is a leftist trait." It's worth noting that *The Organizer's Manual* (see List of Works Cited—Works Without Named Author), which was written by and for leftists, on page 33 portrays leftist ideology as a means of avoiding self-hatred.

In reference to paragraphs 38–41, surrogate activities. A distinction should be made between individual and collective surrogate activities. To take an example, if an individual runs long distances, not as a member of a running club and without expectation of running competitively, and runs more than is necessary for the promotion of health, then he or she engages in a purely individual surrogate activity. But if an individual runs as a member of a running club in competition with other members of the club, then an important part of his or her motive may be to win status among the members of the club. For the club collectively, running is a pure surrogate activity because its only purpose is to give the members of the club an opportunity to experience the power process. But for the individual member of the club running may not be a pure surrogate activity, because its purpose may be, at least in part, to achieve status within the club. This point is important in connection with the discussion of science as a surrogate activity (paragraphs 87–92). Science is, in part, a *collective* surrogate activity, because most individual scientists are motivated to a significant degree by a desire to achieve status among other scientists (which is not the same thing as achieving status in society at large).

In reference to the last paragraph of Note 48. This paragraph may soon lose its validity, because sophisticated computer algorithms are beginning to make individualized manipulation possible without individualized decision-making by human beings.

Postscript (2007) to ISAIF

ISAIF, *Industrial Society and its Future*, has been criticized as "unoriginal," but this misses the point. ISAIF was never intended to be original. Its purpose was to set forth certain points about modern technology in clear and relatively brief form, so that those points could be read and understood by people who would never work their way through a difficult text such as Jacques Ellul's *Technological Society*.

The accusation of unoriginality is in any case irrelevant. Is it important for the future of the world to know whether Ted Kaczynski is original or unoriginal? Obviously not! But it is indeed important for the future of the world to know whether modern technology has us on the road to disaster, whether anything short of revolution can avert that disaster, and whether the political left is an obstacle to revolution. So why have critics, for the most part, ignored the substance of the arguments raised in ISAIF and wasted words on matters of negligible importance, such as the author's putative lack of originality and the defects of his style? Clearly, the critics can't answer the substance of ISAIF's reasoning, so they try to divert their own and others' attention from its arguments by attacking irrelevant aspects of ISAIF.

One doesn't need to be original to recognize that technological progress is taking us down the road to disaster, and that nothing short of the overthrow of the entire technological system will get us off that road. In other words, only by accepting a massive disaster now can we avoid a far worse disaster later. But most of our intellectuals—and here I use that term in a broad sense—prefer not to face up to this frightening dilemma because, after all, they are not very brave, and they find it more comfortable to spend their time perfecting society's solutions to problems left over from the 19th century, such as those of social inequality, colonialism, cruelty to animals, and the like.

I haven't read everything that's been written on the technology problem, and it's possible that ISAIF may have been preceded by some other text that expounded the problem in equally brief and accessible form. But even so it would not follow that ISAIF was superfluous. However familiar its points may be to social scientists, those points still have not come to the attention of many other people who ought to be aware of them. More importantly, the available knowledge on this subject is not being *applied*. I don't think many of our intellectuals nowadays would deny that there *is* a technology problem, but nearly all of them decline to address it. At best they discuss particular problems created by technological progress, such as global warming or the spread of nuclear weapons. The technology problem as a whole is simply ignored.

It follows that the facts about technological progress and its consequences for society cannot be repeated too often. Even the most intelligent people may refuse to face up to a painful truth until it has been drummed into their heads again and again.

If there is anything new in my approach, it is that I've taken revolution seriously as a practical proposition. Many radical environmentalists and "green" anarchists talk of revolution, but as far as I am aware none of them have shown any understanding of how real revolutions come about, nor do they seem to grasp the fact that the exclusive target of revolution must be technology itself, not racism, sexism, or homophobia. A very few serious thinkers have suggested revolution against the technological system; for example, Ellul, in his *Autopsy of Revolution*. But Ellul only dreams of a revolution that would result from a vaguely defined, spontaneous spiritual transformation of society, and he comes very close to admitting that the proposed spiritual transformation is impossible. I on the other hand think it plausible that the preconditions for revolution may be developing in modern society, and I mean a real revolution, not fundamentally different in character from other revolutions that have occurred in the past. But this revolution will not become a reality without a well-defined revolutionary movement guided by suitable leaders—leaders who have a rational understanding of what they are doing, not enraged adolescents acting solely on the basis of emotion.

Excerpt from Letter to D.L. (January 14, 2006)

Dear Mr. D.L.,

I trust you've received my note dated December 16, 2005. Here I will give you my answers to the three questions that you sent me with your letter postmarked November 7, 2005.

First I need to state my conviction that destructiveness toward the natural world is built into technological civilization. It may be feasible to palliate that destructiveness to a limited extent, but in the long run there will be no way of controlling it. Consequently, wild nature, or the biosphere (or whatever you choose to call it), cannot be saved by anything short of the dissolution of technological civilization. It follows that if we want to save the biosphere, then the only really effective actions we can take are those designed to promote the breakdown of technological civilization.

Of course, every civilization breaks down eventually, and technological civilization will do so too. But if technological civilization lasts long enough, then there will be nothing left after it is gone. On the other hand, if technological civilization breaks down soon enough, much will be saved. So the objective must be to bring about the collapse of technological civilization at the earliest possible moment. This point of view underlies my answers to your questions.

To answer your questions in order:

1. (a) You ask what I "see as the long-range goal for those who participate in direct actions in defense of the Earth." I take it you are asking about the long-range goal of ELF, ALF, and those who subscribe approximately to their ideology. Since I am not one of these people, I am not qualified to state their goal for them. But from what I know of this ideological sector, I won't be surprised if most of your respondents state goals that are fuddled, or unrealistic, or both. I also think that the *stated* goals of people who belong to this sector do not necessarily coincide with their *real* goals. I don't doubt that these people *believe* that their stated goals are their real goals, but I would argue that in many cases their real goal is not to save the environment or to protect animals but to satisfy their own psychological needs. See the discussion of leftist psychology in the so-called "Unabomber Manifesto", *Industrial Society and Its Future.*

The foregoing notwithstanding, I speculate that among people who carry out illegal actions in defense of the environment (*not* among animal-rights activists), the stated goals of at least a significant minority do coincide roughly with their real goals. I base this conjecture on the fact that there are very good reasons, connected with the welfare of all human beings, for protecting our environment. The system's response to environmental problems has been feeble at best, so it is only to be expected that some people should grow sufficiently worried, frustrated, or angry to become "extremists" in defense of the environment.

I would also speculate that the people who work "in the field", that is, the people who repeatedly take the risk of engaging personally in illegal actions, have (on average) a stronger commitment to accomplishing practical results and are less interested in ideology than are activists who adopt primarily political methods. A relative lack of interest in ideology would suggest a more genuine commitment to defending the environment; people seeking mainly to satisfy their own psychological needs would be more likely to develop elaborate ideological rationalizations.

(b) You ask where I "see things going for the environmental and animal-rights movements." Here I assume you are referring not to the legal, conventional movements as represented for example by the Wilderness Society, the Sierra Club, or the Humane Society, but to the extreme movements represented by ELF and ALF.

I don't have any detailed knowledge of these movements, and even if I did I wouldn't venture to make any *specific* predictions about their future. In general terms I predict that these movements will never accomplish anything substantial. The extreme environmental movement may contribute to some palliation of modern society's abuse of the environment, but will not have a decisive effect. The extreme animal-rights movement probably will succeed only to the extent that a tendency toward more humane treatment of animals may already be predetermined by powerful social trends in modern society. There certainly is in our society a long-term trend in the direction of a more compassionate attitude toward animals. Even conservatives advocate more humane treatment of animals. See George F. Will's column in *Newsweek*, 7/18/05, page 66. It's true that there are economic forces that push in the opposite direction, and I suppose it's conceivable, though not likely, that the extreme animal-rights movement might tilt the balance in favor of humane treatment and against the economic incentives for ruthless exploitation of animals. But even if this happens it will not be of decisive importance for the future of the world.

I should add at this point that I'm not particularly interested in animal rights. Of course, I do not like to know, for example, that many chickens spend their lives in cages so small that the birds can't even turn around, but this is not a matter of special concern to me. As I've already implied, I don't think the question of animal rights will be of much significance for the overall development of modern society in the years to come.

So, in summary, I see the environmental and animal-rights movements as futile, at least with respect to any issues that are of fundamental importance for the future of the world. As I indicated at the beginning of this letter, *the* fundamental issue is the survival or collapse of technological civilization.

(c) You ask whether I see any hope for the extreme environmental and animal-rights movements. No, I do not. The reason why I see the futility of these movements as incurable is that they are under the domination of what the Unabomber Manifesto calls "the left", or what some others have called "the adversary culture". (See Paul Hollander's book, *The Survival of the Adversary Culture.*) Roughly, "the left" comprises people who are fixated on such issues as racism, sexism, neocolonialism, gay rights, animal rights, indigenous people's rights, etc., etc. These people like to think of themselves as rebels or revolutionaries, but they wouldn't really want to overturn the existing structure of society. They have in fact achieved a relatively comfortable adjustment to the present society, which allows them to satisfy their psychological needs by playing at rebellion as long as they stay within certain limits (of course, not all of them do so), and as long as they espouse causes that are consistent with the well-being of technological society. Unquestionably, technological society is benefited by the suppression of racism, sexism, homophobia, etc., and by moderate measures for protection of the environment. On the other hand, if technological civilization collapses, many, many people will die, and the survivors will have to live under conditions that will seem exceedingly harsh to those accustomed to the soft life of modern society. In the struggle for survival, no one will care about the leftists' favorite issues, such as gender equality, kindness to animals, or the right of homosexuals to marry.

Thus the leftists would have nothing to gain, and a great deal to lose, through the collapse of technological civilization, and most leftists—even including many of those who like to *talk* about such a collapse—would not actually want to see technological civilization break down.[1] Furthermore, the values of the left are essentially the soft values of modern society: women, homosexuals, and animals are to be protected, poor people are to be cared for, workers are to be given easy conditions and decent wages, etc., etc. A movement dominated by these soft values could never take the frankly brutal and reckless measures needed to bring down the technoindustrial system, nor would such a movement be prepared to accept the harsh consequences of the collapse of the system.

No doubt there are some individuals, and possibly even whole factions in the environmental/animal-rights movement who genuinely do want to see the collapse of technological civilization, would be willing to accept the frightening consequences of such a collapse, and might even be prepared to take the brutal measures needed to bring it about. But scattered individuals and small factions cannot constitute an effective revolutionary force as long as they remain part of a movement that is dominated by the left and its values.

The revolutionary pretensions of the left are good for a laugh. What isn't so funny is the fact that the existence of the left serves to impede the emergence of a *real* revolutionary movement. Leftists love causes—*any* causes, as long as they don't have a specifically right-wing character. So as soon as any movement of resistance begins to form, leftists come swarming to it in droves until the movement becomes swamped with leftists, is absorbed into the "adversary culture", and is thereby rendered ineffectual. The history of Earth First! provides a nice example of this phenomenon. Martha F. Lee has documented the process in her book, *Earth First!: Environmental Apocalypse*.

Thus, those who are seriously interested in saving wild nature must rigorously separate themselves from the left—that includes separating themselves from ELF, ALF, the green anarchists, the anarchoprimitivists, and so forth—and they must form a new movement of their own, which will have to take measures to exclude leftists. The new movement will need to discard the soft values of the left and adopt hard values. It will have to place the highest value on courage, skill, effort, endurance—and on freedom, but not the pampered freedom of the modern man or woman to whom society gives a long leash. Instead, the movement must value the self-reliant freedom of

1 "When the old order begins to fall apart, many of the vociferous men of words, who prayed so long for the day, are in a funk. The first glimpse of the face of anarchy frightens them out of their wits." Eric Hoffer, *The True Believer*, §110.

the rugged survivalist, and it will have to *glory* in the hard life to be expected following the dissolution of technological civilization.

(d) You ask how, "ultimately", I see things ending up. I think I've answered that question already: If technological civilization breaks down in the relatively near future, then much will be saved. But if technological civilization lasts too long, then, when it does eventually break down, there will be nothing left to save.

2. (a) You ask how I became interested in the animal-rights/environmental movement. As I've already made clear, I'm not interested in the animal-rights/environmental movement, except to the extent that I view it as an adversary to be resisted.

(b) You ask about my "personal background (education, family, political beliefs, influence, etc.)." Education: B.A., mathematics, Harvard, 1962. Ph.D., mathematics, University of Michigan, 1967. Family: working-class to lower middle-class. Political beliefs: If the term "politics" is construed in a narrow sense, then I'm not interested in politics. If the term is more broadly construed, then my political beliefs are those that have already been outlined in this letter. Influences: No comment.

3. (a) You are perhaps a wee bit careless in telling your respondents that their opinions about "illegal direct actions" "may be freely expressed" and are "protected by the First Amendment." Expressions of opinion about illegal action are protected by the First Amendment only if they do not constitute actual *incitement* of illegal action. See *Yates v. United States*, 354 U.S. 298, 313-334 (1957); *Nowak v. United States*, 356 U.S. 660, 666-67 (1958); *Kingsley Corp. v. Regents of U. of N.Y.*, 360 U.S. 684, 689 (1959); *Scales v. United States*, 367 U.S. 203 (1961); *Noto v. United States*, 367 U.S. 290, 297-98 (1961); *Carroll v. Commissioners of Princess Anne*, 393 U.S. 175, 180 (1968); *Brandenburg v. Ohio*, 395 U.S. 444, 447 (1969); *Hess v. Indiana*, 414 U.S. 105, 108-09 (1973); *Ashcroft v. Free Speech Coalition*, 535 U.S. 234, 253 (2002). The line between incitement and protected expression of opinion about illegal action is difficult to define precisely, and it won't be surprising if some of the opinions expressed by your respondents constitute, in the eyes of some people, incitement of illegal action.

Here I will be very careful to avoid incitement, and will stay well within the area protected by the First Amendment.

(b) You ask whether "illegal actions are an acceptable way of trying to change behaviors relating to the environment and nonhuman animals". I doubt that illegal direct actions, on the scale currently practiced, are highly effective in changing behaviors related to the environment and nonhuman animals. I do think that illegal direct actions may turn out to be a necessary part of a revolutionary program designed to bring down technological civilization.

(c) You ask how I would justify actions that are against the law.

Law is a code of behavior designed to preserve the structure of a given society. If one believes that a society should *not* be preserved, then one has no reason to obey its laws—provided that one is willing to accept the personal risk involved in breaking the law.

Sincerely yours,
Ted Kaczynski

If EF! Had Been Around During World War II... (2001)

President Franklin D. Roosevelt, at his desk in the Oval Office, was gazing thoughtfully at a sheaf of paper that he held in his hands.

"General," he said, "after much soul-searching I've become convinced that we have a moral obligation to accept this proposal. A detailed plan for winning the war without violence and bloodshed is not something that we can allow ourselves to cast aside. We have to give these people a chance to show what they can do."

General Marshall shook his head skeptically.

"I don't know, Mr. President. Disbanding the entire United States Army and replacing it with an army trained by these people—that's a pretty drastic measure. It might not work."

"Nothing ventured, nothing gained," the President replied. "Besides, it would be immoral to use violence against the Nazis. Two wrongs can never make a right! And you know how it is in war. No matter how careful we try to be, not only soldiers are killed but many innocent civilians as well, even children. No, General, we cannot participate in the crime of violent warfare!"

General Marshall shrugged his shoulders in resignation.

"Alright, Mr. President. You're the Commander in Chief. If those are your orders..."

"Those are my orders, General."

***

The armored column had halted, and the tanks stood in the dusty road with their engines idling as Captain Arschenküsser talked with Colonel Fleischhacker over a field telephone. Private Kleinermann, with his head and shoulders sticking out of the turret of the lead tank, was able to hear the Captain's end of the conversation.

"It gives here zumting very strange, Herr Oberst Fleischhacker. Der Amerikaners ist in der mittle of der road about a qvarter of a mile ahead of us dug in. I have dem mit der binoculars examined, und dey have der Amerikanischer flag from a schtick flying, und right under der Amerikanischer flag have dey anudder flag flying, dat I never before seen have."

The Captain paused to listen for a moment to Colonel Fleischhacker. Then he answered:

"Was ist das, Herr Oberst? Sie fragen mich, warum ich gebrochenes Englisch und nicht gutes Deutsch spreche? Natürlich, Herr Oberst, werden die Leser dieser Geschichte nicht verstehen, wenn ich Deutsch spreche. Deshalb, Herr Oberst, spreche ich mit Verlaub gebrochenes Englisch."

"Dis udder flag of der Amerikaners," the Captain continued, "has on it der picture of ein clenched fist, der symbol of fanatical defiance! Derefore ve can expecting desperate resistance! A hard ge-fought battle! But der ting, vhat I do not understand, Herr Oberst, is dat I do not by der Amerikaners any veapons see. No Maschineguns, no artillery, no rifles. It must be zum kind of trick. Ve vill have to be very careful, so dat ve do not become by der Yankees in ein ambush ge-trapped."

The Captain listened again to the Colonel for a few moments and then concluded,

"Ja, Herr Oberst! Ve vill advance mit der greatest caution! Heil Hitler!"

He hung up the phone and climbed onto the lead tank, where he crouched just in front of Private Kleinermann's turret, scanning the American position with his binoculars while the tanks slowly advanced. As the distance between the tanks and the Americans decreased, an expression of astonishment and incredulity spread over the Captain's face. By the time the lead tank had stopped within ten feet of the Americans, he found himself flatly unable to believe what he was seeing. He turned to Private Kleinermann and looked him hard in the eyes.

"Gemeiner Kleinermann, am I from der delirium suffering, or do you zee vhat I zee?"

"Vhat I zee, Herr Hauptmann Arschenküsser, ist a lot of peoples buried up to der neck in der middle of der road, und a lot of udder peoples lying across der road mit der arms und der legs by strange contraptions of concrete and steel held. Und dey are all along der road as far as der eye can zee."

"Komm, Gemeiner Kleinermann," said the Captain, "ve must closer looking."

The two men climbed down off the tank. The Americans' clenched-fist flag was dangling from its stick right in front of them. The Captain grasped it by one corner and held it up so that its design could be seen. Beneath the clenched fist was the legend, "Earth First! 103rd Regiment." The Captain, puzzled, lifted his coal-scuttle helmet and scratched his head.

"Was ist das? I have never ge-heard of such a regiment."

The Captain and the Private stepped gingerly among the prostrate bodies, examining the contraptions that held their limbs.

"Maybe, Herr Hauptmann"—the Private pointed his right index finger at his temple and spun it rapidly in a small circle—"maybe dey are verrückt?"

"Ja, Gemeiner Kleinermann, dey must be verrückt!"

The Captain placed his fists on his hips with his arms akimbo and surveyed the scene with disgust.

"Verdammt! Dey are blocking completely der road, und der vay dey are mit dese contraptions ge-chained, it vould take veeks to cut dem all loose und get dem out of der vay! Komm, Gemeiner Kleinermann. Ve must der headqvarters telephonieren und asking der Oberst vhat to do about dis."

The two soldiers goose-stepped back along the road to the field telephone, and Captain Arschenküsser rang up headquarters again. To Colonel Fleischhacker he briefly outlined what he had found and asked what steps he ought to take. Private Kleinermann watched the Captain turn pale as he listened to the Colonel's reply. The Colonel was shouting so loudly that the private could catch fragments of his tirade even at the distance of ten feet from the phone.

"...Schweinehund!..Dummkopf!... Du bist ein Esel!..."

"I'm sorry, Herr Oberst," mumbled the Captain. "It isn't my fault, Herr Oberst... please forgive me, Herr Oberst... I vill do mein best, Herr Oberst..."

"...I vill have you shot!...Dummkopf!...Schweinehund!...Esel!"

"...Ja, Herr Oberst... I understand, Herr Oberst... ...immediately, Herr Oberst!... Heil Hitler!"

The Captain slammed the telephone down and took off running toward the head of the column, galumping along in his heavy jackboots. As he neared the lead tanks he began shouting:

"Vorwärts!... Vorwärts!... Vorwärts!"

The powerful engines revved and roared, and the tanks lurched ahead. Private Kleinermann covered his eyes with his hands. It was just too horrible to watch.

***

Water Lily and Daffodil were sitting disconsolately in the dust. The dense barbed-wire entanglements that surrounded the camp shut out their view of the vast, flat plains of Kansas that stretched away to the horizon in every direction. At the top of a tall pole in front of the commandant's office, a flag stirred lazily in the breeze. Tired of saying nothing, Daffodil broke the silence.

"I hate that flag," he said.

Water Lily glanced at the swastika banner.

"Yeah," she answered, "I hate it too." After a pause she added, "I guess we lost big."

"We sure did," said Daffodil, "We lost *real* big. Sometimes I think we should have fought the Nazis with guns, even though it would have been immoral."

"You're right," said Water Lily. "We should have. But now it's too late."

Letter to AJODA (September 14, 1998)

Dear Mr. X,

In all my years in Montana I never saw but one badger, probably because they frequent the open prairies at lower elevations, whereas I spent my time in the wooded areas and the high mountains. The one badger I did see I met while walking home from a run along Humbug Contour Road. He was walking along the road in the opposite direction and I encountered him as I came around a bend. As soon as he saw me he scampered down off the road and took cover under a log. I went down to get a closer look at him. Instead of cowering or running away as most animals would have done, he challenged me by opening his jaws and thrusting himself in my direction with a hissing sound. He was a beautiful animal!

I found your magazine mildly entertaining, but I will tell you frankly that I think you would have accomplished more if you had devoted the whole thing to badger lore. It is a waste of time to write about the squabbles of people like Bob Black and Murray Chinbook or whatever his name is. What they do or say doesn't matter. Forests are being cut to feed the growth of an evil system, species are being exterminated, geneticists are meddling with the very basis of life, our society gets ever more mechanized and inhuman—and the anarchists, meanwhile, are quibbling about the morality of a trick that Bob Black played on someone. So who cares?

As far as I can judge from what I have learned of it, the American anarchist movement is absolutely useless. The anarchist journals that people have sent me have just been filled with petty doctrinal squabbles. If you guys were serious, you would fill your journals instead with discussions of the *practical* steps that have to be taken to bring down the system, of how to build an *effective* movement with a *practical* orientation.

That the anarchists are accomplishing nothing is proved by the fact that the media don't make propaganda against you (as they do against gangs, cults, militias), you're not being arrested, harassed, etc. The system just ignores you, as it can afford to do because you're no danger to it.

I won't take American anarchism seriously until I start reading in the newspaper about how vile, dangerous, immoral etc. the anarchists are, or when I hear that the FBI is giving you a hard time, or something along those lines.

Okay, I apologize for the harshness of these remarks, but I really wish you guys would get off your lazy asses and start taking effective action.

Best Regards,
Ted Kaczynski

Letter to Green Anarchy (August 6, 2001)

Dear *Green Anarchy*:

I see from *Green Anarchy*, No. 6, page 7, that Jesus says the Zapatistas are resisting modernization. If that's true, then they had better get rid of Subcomandante Marcos, ¡muy pronto! The good Subcomandante is no opponent of modernization. Here are some quotes from a speech that he gave during the Zapatista's recent march on Mexico City:

"If we don't already have enough money for medicine, now they will be taking another bit out of our wages.... .

"The economic packages... mean nothing to us but more taxes, price increases, salary reductions, more unemployment, fewer work benefits, lower budgets for education, less housing, fewer services, less food, fewer lands, fewer hospitals, fewer doctors, less medicine.

"...[O]n what used to be our land, we put up airports for the new bosses. But we will never travel in a plane. Similarly, we build highways, and we will never have an automobile. We build entertainment centers, and we will never have access to them. We put up shopping centers, and we will never have money to shop in them. We build urban zones with all the services, and we will only see them from afar. We erect modern hotels, and we will never stay in them.

"In short, we are putting up a world which excludes us.... .

"You made the house, you put in the electricity, the water, the plumbing. You paved the street. You planted the garden. You built the furniture. You painted the walls. You set the tables. You got the food. You prepared the meal.

"And you are left outside. Because someone else came in and occupied the house.

"Someone else is the one whose life is illuminated. Someone else is the one who cleans himself up; the one who goes in the vehicle; the one who uses the furniture; the one who enjoys our work; the one who is fed. ...

"The one which has the light, prosperity, progress, joy, hope is theirs, those who, being few, have everything.

"The street and the countryside are for us. They call our destitution home. ...

"You will leave school and you will find there are no jobs, and if there are any, they are poorly paid. Graduating from a public school is good for nothing but third-rate employment."

(From speech by Subcomandante Marcos at National Polytechnic Institute, Zacatenco, Mexico, March, 2001, as quoted in English translation in *Food & Water Journal*, Summer, 2001, pages 24-27.)

It's clear what Subcomandante Marcos is driving at, and it isn't an end to modernity. He just wants the poor people to have their fair share of the technological pie. Undoubtedly, poor people *do* deserve their share of the pie—if you accept that the pie should exist at all. But if you don't believe that there should be any electricity, plumbing, modern medicine, schools, or jobs, then it makes no sense to say that poor people ought to have a share of these things.

It's an old, sad, often-repeated story: True and genuine popular rebellion is taken over by sophisticated leftist intellectuals—in this case Subcomandante Marx, I mean Marcos, and his cronies—who manipulate it, betray it, and pervert it to their own ends. The leftists have done this again and again. When will people ever learn? When will you, Green Anarchists, ever learn?

Ted Kaczynski

P.S. You can print this letter, if you like. —TJK.

Ship of Fools (1999)

Once upon a time, the captain and the mates of a ship grew so vain of their seamanship, so full of hubris and so impressed with themselves, that they went mad. They turned the ship north and sailed until they met with icebergs and dangerous floes, and they kept sailing north into more and more perilous waters, solely in order to give themselves opportunities to perform ever-more-brilliant feats of seamanship.

As the ship reached higher and higher latitudes, the passengers and crew became increasingly uncomfortable. They began quarreling among themselves and complaining of the conditions under which they lived.

"Shiver me timbers," said an able seaman, "if this ain't the worst voyage I've ever been on. The deck is slick with ice; when I'm on lookout the wind cuts through me jacket like a knife; every time I reef the foresail I blamed-near freeze me fingers; and all I get for it is a miserable five shillings a month!"

"You think *you* have it bad!" said a lady passenger. "I can't sleep at night for the cold. Ladies on this ship don't get as many blankets as the men. It isn't fair!"

A Mexican sailor chimed in: "¡Chingado! I'm only getting half the wages of the Anglo seamen. We need plenty of food to keep us warm in this climate, and I'm not getting my share; the Anglos get more. And the worst of it is that the mates always give me orders in English instead of Spanish."

"I have more reason to complain than anybody," said an American Indian sailor. "If the palefaces hadn't robbed me of my ancestral lands, I wouldn't even be on this ship, here among the icebergs and arctic winds. I would just be paddling a canoe on a nice, placid lake. I deserve compensation. At the very least, the captain should let me run a crap game so that I can make some money."

The bosun spoke up: "Yesterday the first mate called me a 'fruit' just because I suck cocks. I have a right to suck cocks without being called names for it!"

"It's not only humans who are mistreated on this ship," interjected an animal-lover among the passengers, her voice quivering with indignation. "Why, last week I saw the second mate kick the ship's dog twice!"

One of the passengers was a college professor. Wringing his hands he exclaimed,

"All this is just awful! It's immoral! It's racism, sexism, speciesism, homophobia, and exploitation of the working class! It's discrimination! We must have social justice: Equal wages for the Mexican sailor, higher wages for all sailors, compensation for the Indian, equal blankets for the ladies, a guaranteed right to suck cocks, and no more kicking the dog!"

"Yes, yes!" shouted the passengers. "Aye-aye!" shouted the crew. "It's discrimination! We have to demand our rights!"

The cabin boy cleared his throat.

"Ahem. You all have good reasons to complain. But it seems to me that what we really have to do is get this ship turned around and headed back south, because if we keep going north we're sure to be wrecked sooner or later, and then your wages, your blankets, and your right to suck cocks won't do you any good, because we'll all drown."

But no one paid any attention to him, because he was only the cabin boy.

The captain and the mates, from their station on the poop deck, had been watching and listening. Now they smiled and winked at one another, and at a gesture from the captain the third mate came down from the poop deck, sauntered over to where the passengers and crew were gathered, and shouldered his way in amongst them. He put a very serious expression on his face and spoke thusly:

"We officers have to admit that some really inexcusable things have been happening on this ship. We hadn't realized how bad the situation was until we heard your complaints. We are men of good will and want to do right by you. But—well—the captain is rather conservative and set in his ways, and may have to be prodded a bit before he'll make any substantial changes. My personal opinion is that if you would protest vigorously—but always peacefully and without violating any of the ship's rules—you would shake the captain out of his inertia and force him to address the problems of which you so justly complain."

Having said this, the third mate headed back toward the poop deck. As he went, the passengers and crew called after him, "Moderate! Reformer! Goody-liberal! Captain's stooge!" But they nevertheless did as he said. They gathered in a body before the poop deck, shouted insults at the officers, and demanded their rights: "I want higher wages and better working conditions," cried the able seaman. "Equal blankets for women," cried the lady passenger. "I want to receive my orders in Spanish," cried the Mexican sailor. "I want the right to run a crap game," cried the Indian sailor. "I don't want to be called a fruit," cried the bosun. "No more kicking the dog," cried the animal lover. "Revolution now," cried the professor.

The captain and the mates huddled together and conferred for several minutes, winking, nodding, and smiling at one another all the while. Then the captain stepped to the front of the poop deck and, with a great show of benevolence, announced that the able seaman's wages would be raised to six shillings a month; the Mexican sailor's wages would be raised to two-thirds the wages of an Anglo seaman, and the order to reef the foresail would be given in Spanish; lady passengers would receive one more blanket; the Indian sailor would be allowed to run a crap game on Saturday nights; the bosun wouldn't be called a fruit as long as he kept his cocksucking strictly private; and the dog wouldn't be kicked unless he did something really naughty, such as stealing food from the galley.

The passengers and crew celebrated these concessions as a great victory, but by next morning, they were again feeling dissatisfied.

"Six shillings a month is a pittance, and I still freeze me fingers when I reef the foresail," grumbled the able seaman. "I'm still not getting the same wages as the Anglos, or enough food for this climate," said the Mexican sailor. "We women still don't have enough blankets to keep us warm," said the lady passenger. The other crewmen and passengers voiced similar complaints, and the professor egged them on.

When they were done, the cabin boy spoke up—louder this time so that the others could not so easily ignore him:

"It's really terrible that the dog gets kicked for stealing a bit of bread from the galley, and that women don't have equal blankets, and that the able seaman gets his fingers frozen; and I don't see why the bosun shouldn't suck cocks if he wants to. But look how thick the icebergs are now, and how the wind blows harder and harder! We've got to turn this ship back toward the south, because if we keep going north we'll be wrecked and drowned."

"Oh, yes!" said the bosun, "It's just so *awful* that we keep heading north. But why should I have to keep my cocksucking in the closet? Why should I be called a fruit? Ain't I as good as everyone else?"

"Sailing north is *terrible*," said the lady passenger. "But don't you see? That's exactly why women need more blankets to keep them warm. I demand equal blankets for women now!"

"It's quite true," said the professor, "that sailing to the north imposes great hardships on all of us. But changing course toward the south would be unrealistic. You can't turn back the clock. We must find a mature way of dealing with the situation."

"Look," said the cabin boy, "If we let those four madmen up on the poop deck have their way, we'll all be drowned. If we ever get the ship out of danger, then we can worry about working conditions, blankets for women, and the right to suck cocks. But first we've got to get this vessel turned around. If a few of us get together, make a plan, and show some courage, we can save ourselves. It wouldn't take many of us—six or eight would do. We could charge the poop, chuck those lunatics overboard, and turn the ship to the south."

The professor elevated his nose and said sternly, "I don't believe in violence. It's immoral."

"It's unethical *ever* to use violence," said the bosun.

"I'm terrified of violence," said the lady passenger.

The captain and the mates had been watching and listening all the while. At a signal from the captain, the third mate stepped down to the main deck. He went about among the passengers and crew, telling them that there were still many problems on the ship.

"We have made much progress," he said, "But much remains to be done. Working conditions for the able seaman are still hard, the Mexican still isn't getting the same wages as the Anglos, the women still don't have quite as many blankets as the men, the Indian's Saturday-night crap game is a paltry compensation for his lost lands, it's unfair to the bosun that he has to keep his cocksucking in the closet, and the dog still gets kicked at times.

"I think the captain needs to be prodded again. It would help if you all would put on another protest—as long as it remains nonviolent."

As the third mate walked back toward the stern, the passengers and crew shouted insults after him, but they nevertheless did what he said and gathered in front of the poop deck for another protest. They ranted and raved and brandished their fists, and they even threw a rotten egg at the captain (which he skillfully dodged).

After hearing their complaints, the captain and the mates huddled for a conference, during which they winked and grinned broadly at one another. Then the captain stepped to the front of the poop deck and announced that the able seaman would be given gloves to keep his fingers warm, the Mexican sailor would receive wages equal to three-fourths the wages of an Anglo seaman, the women would receive yet another blanket, the Indian sailor could run a crap game on Saturday *and* Sunday nights, the bosun would be allowed to suck cocks publicly after dark, and no one could kick the dog without special permission from the captain.

The passengers and crew were ecstatic over this great revolutionary victory, but by the next morning they were again feeling dissatisfied and began grumbling about the same old hardships.

The cabin boy this time was getting angry.

"You damn fools!" he shouted. "Don't you see what the captain and the mates are doing? They're keeping you occupied with your trivial grievances about blankets and wages and the dog being kicked so that you won't think about what is *really* wrong with this ship—that it's getting farther and farther to the north and we're all going to be drowned. If just a few of you would come to your senses, get together, and charge the poop deck, we could turn this ship around and save ourselves. But all you do is whine about petty little issues like working conditions and crap games and the right to suck cocks."

The passengers and crew were incensed.

"Petty!!" cried the Mexican, "Do you think it's reasonable that I get only three-fourths the wages of an Anglo sailor? Is that *petty*?"

"How can you call *my* grievance trivial?" shouted the bosun. "Don't you know how humiliating it is to be called a fruit?"

"Kicking the dog is not a 'petty little issue!'" screamed the animal-lover. "It's heartless, cruel, and brutal!"

"Alright then," answered the cabin boy. "These issues are not petty and trivial. Kicking the dog is cruel and brutal and it is humiliating to be called a fruit. But in comparison to our *real* problem—in comparison to the fact that the ship is still heading north—your grievances *are* petty and trivial, because if we don't get this ship turned around soon we're all going to drown."

"Fascist!" said the professor.

"Counterrevolutionary!" said the lady passenger. And all of the passengers and crew chimed in one after another, calling the cabin boy a fascist and a counterrevolutionary. They pushed him away and went back to grumbling about wages, and about blankets for women, and about the right to suck cocks, and about how the dog was treated. The ship kept sailing north, and after a while it was crushed between two icebergs and everyone drowned.

Letter to John Zerzan (December 20, 2001)

Dear John,

In your letter of December 10, 2001, you criticized my exclusive focus on technology, saying that we ought to see "all of the totality."

"Totality" is a fine-sounding word, but you fail to explain its practical application in the present context. Suppose you want to disable a bulldozer. If you see the bulldozer in all its totality, you will recognize that some parts of it are not essential to the functioning of the whole machine, whereas other parts *are* essential—the machine can't function without them. Consequently, if you see the bulldozer in all its totality you will know that you had best ignore its inessential parts and concentrate your efforts exclusively on destroying the essential parts.

You asked, "do you not feel it is at all important, for example, that half the population is constantly subjected to objectification and the threat of violence?"

Do you, John, not feel it is at all important, for example, that some sixty thousand people a year are killed in traffic accidents in the U.S., and many thousands more are permanently disabled? But what would you say to a revolutionary movement that claimed to want to overthrow the existing system, yet devoted the greater part of its resources to the prevention of traffic accidents? I know what *I* would say to them. I would say:

"If you think that preventing traffic accidents is more important than overthrowing the system, then just concentrate on traffic accidents and stop pretending to be revolutionaries. Leave revolution to those who are serious about it.

"On the other hand, if you think that overthrowing the system is more important than preventing traffic accidents, then you had better forget about traffic accidents and concentrate exclusively on overthrowing the system, because overthrowing the system is an overwhelmingly difficult task, and if you squander your resources on preventing traffic accidents you won't make any progress toward overthrowing the system."

And that's pretty much what I say to you, John. If you think that women's issues, black people's issues, gay rights, animal rights, etc., etc., etc., etc., etc. are more important than getting rid of the technosystem then I suggest you confine your attention to those issues and leave the technology problem to the people who are serious about it. By meddling in the struggle against technology you only muddy the waters, confuse the issues, and thereby make things more difficult for those who are fully committed to getting rid of the technosystem.

On the other hand, if you think that getting rid of the technosystem is more important than all those other issues, then you had better just forget about the other issues. The technosystem is big, tough, and powerful while we are relatively weak. If we disperse our limited resources among a dozen different causes, we will never be able to accomplish anything against the technosystem.

This is only the short answer to your point. I have plenty more to say in this connection, and will say much of it in later articles.

If you haven't done so already, you might want to read my article "Ship of Fools."

Best regards,
Ted Kaczynski

Succinct Book Review (March 10, 2019)

Ernesto "Che" Guevara, *Diario de Bolivia*, **Ediciones B, Barcelona, 1996.**

A well-known, romantic-looking portrait of Che Guevara has been widely disseminated by leftists, who generally regard him as a revolutionary hero. But the truth is that Guevara was utterly incompetent as a revolutionary. This is demonstrated by his own account of his bungled attempt to start a revolution in Bolivia. The diary (here under review) that Guevara kept from November 1966 to October 1967 reveals that he made at least three amateurish mistakes, any one of which by itself would likely have been fatal to his attempt at revolution.

First, the personnel of Guevara's guerrilla band were carelessly selected. Guevara should have realized that he needed, at the very least, a solid core of tested, reliable people to form the backbone of his band, and that it was important to make sure that the other members of the band were at least adequate for his purposes. As it was, he embarked on his guerrilla campaign with a random collection of volunteers who were incapable of any high level of discipline and organization, and whose revolutionary commitment was so weak that most of those who were captured readily gave information to the authorities. The predictable result was that Guevara got a lot of people killed to no purpose—including himself.

Second, the region in which Guevara tried to conduct his guerrilla war was largely wild, though there were human habitations and agricultural plots scattered here and there. Since none of the would-be revolutionaries were familiar with the terrain, a modicum of common sense would have dictated that before the whole guerrilla band set off into the wilds a small party of two or three should have spent a year or so covertly scouting the territory, so that when the guerrilleros began their campaign they would have competent guides. Because this was not done, Guevara and his band could only blunder around confusedly in the unfamiliar terrain.

Third, it is generally recognized that an attempt at revolution can succeed only when conditions are ripe for it. Before any guerrilla band had been recruited, a few revolutionary agents should have circulated among the peasants, talking with them to ascertain how they would be likely to react in the event of an uprising. But Che Guevara had a crack-brained theory that conditions didn't need to be ripe for revolution; he claimed that guerrilla fighters could start a revolution at any time, if only "the people" were shown that "social wrongs" would not be "redressed by civil means alone."[1] Of course, it didn't work. As Guevara wrote in his diary (page 134), "the peasant base still is not developing; though it appears that by means of the terror campaign we've planned we will secure the neutrality of the majority. Their support will come later." But the guerrilleros never did win the support of the peasants, and that by itself was enough to ensure that their "revolution" would be nothing but a ridiculous fiasco.

It's safe to say that very few leftists will ever take the trouble to read Che Guevara's Bolivian diary, and even if they did read it they would continue to romanticize him as a revolutionary hero, because the left today runs almost entirely on the basis of emotion, with little guidance from rational calculation.

NOTE

1. Guevara, Che, *On Guerrilla Warfare*, Frederick A. Praeger, Inc., Publisher, New York, second printing, 1962, p. 4: "One does not necessarily have to wait for a revolutionary situation to arise; it can be created."

A Halloween Story (December 11, 2011)

It was a Sunday afternoon in late October, and the University of Michigan's zoology department was nearly deserted. Professor Mortimer was taking advantage of the peace and quiet to work on his magnum opus, *Bats of the Great Lakes Region: Their Anatomy, Physiology, and Behavior.* His concentration was broken by a knock at his door.

"Come in," he said.

The door opened and a tall, lean stranger stepped into the office, followed by a man with a shambling gait, vacant eyes, and ill-fitting clothes who carried a large attaché case.

"Professor Mortimer," said the stranger. His penetrating gaze made the professor slightly uncomfortable.

"What can I do for you?" asked the latter.

"You are one of the world's best-known chiropterologists."

The professor warmed with gratified vanity.

"Yes," he confessed with a self-satisfied smile, "I believe I have a generally favorable reputation among my colleagues."

"I have something to show you, professor."

"Oh? What is it?"

In a foreign language with which the professor was unfamiliar, the stranger spoke to his peculiar companion; his tone was dull but authoritative:

"Ignacio. Pon el maletín sobre la mesa."

The acolyte approached the professor's desk awkwardly and placed the attaché case upon it.

"Ignacio. Ábrelo."

The queer fellow opened the attaché case and laid it out flat, then stood staring at it stupidly.

"Ignacio," said the stranger, pointing to a corner of the office, "Siéntate en el rincón."

Ignacio shambled over to the corner, turned his back to the wall, and flopped down onto the floor. There he sat gazing vacantly into space, his shoulders sagging and his legs stretched straight out in front of him.

The stranger pointed with his open hand toward the attaché case, which was filled with thick stacks of paper.

"The product of twenty years of research!" he announced.

"On what subject?"

"Vampire bats."

In the course of his career Professor Mortimer had occasionally been approached by crackpots who insisted on expounding to him some addled theory about bats—usually vampire bats—and he had an uneasy feeling that the stranger was one of them. He was tempted to show him out of the office forthwith, but there was something oddly impressive about the man that made him hesitate. So he merely said in an irritable tone,

"I really don't have time to read through all this."

"Very well, I will give you a brief oral summary. But first..."—the stranger was staring intently at the professor— "But first... have you perhaps seen me before?"

Professor Mortimer studied the stranger's face. There was something in it that held his attention. Yes, maybe he *had* seen the man before. But where? Then suddenly it came to him:

"Abel Osigul!" he exclaimed.

"That is correct, professor. I am Abel Osigul."

"What on earth happened to you? Twenty years ago you were one of the best students I ever had. I do remember that you were especially interested in vampire bats. You were about to begin a Ph.D. thesis on that subject, and then... you disappeared. Where have you been?"

"I've been in the wildest corners of Argentina and Paraguay, where I have made discoveries. Astounding discoveries!"

By this time Professor Mortimer was intensely interested. Abel Osigul was no crackpot.

"I traveled to Argentina, of course, to study vampire bats in preparation for my doctoral dissertation. I went through the usual routine, did all the things that Ph.D. students in mammalogy are expected to do. But one thing troubled me. In the course of my studies I had heard persistent rumors of a remote region on the borders of Argentina and Paraguay in which vampire bats were abnormally abundant, large, and voracious. As you know, professor, I am a perfectionist. My research would have been imperfect if I had not visited the region in question to determine how much, if any, truth there was in the rumors concerning its vampire bats. Consequently, I had to make my way there at any cost.

"Unfortunately, the region was not only inaccessible but was inhabited by the Chabaraní, one of the few remaining tribes to have preserved complete independence from civilization, and so warlike and aggressive that to intrude upon their territory with anything less than a well-armed regiment was said to be virtually suicidal. And any regiment would have perished in attempting to struggle through the vast, fetid swamps that surrounded the country of the Chabaraní.

"I made extensive inquiries, studied old accounts of explorers, travelers, and missionaries, and found that beyond their bloodthirstiness almost nothing was known about the Chabaraní. In 1921 the anthropologist Holmberg departed for their territory with three assistants, intending to carry out an ethnographic study. Some ten months later, alone, grotesquely emaciated, and with his clothing in tatters, he staggered into a frontier settlement. He was hopelessly insane, able only to babble incoherent stories of human sacrifices and unspeakable rites.

"Despite the risk, I had no alternative: In order to complete my research I had to trespass upon the territory of the Chabaraní. Accordingly, I set out from Buenos Aires with a single intrepid companion.

"You are a scientist, Professor Mortimer. You are interested not in adventure stories but in scientific facts. Therefore I will pass over the astonishing hardships and dangers that we had to surmount, and will limit myself to outlining the scientific findings of our twenty years among the Chabaraní.

"As you know, rabies is a disease that originated in the Old World and was transmitted to the New, most likely through dogs brought by Europeans at the time of the Spanish conquest. The disease eventually infected bats, which thereafter became important carriers of rabies. Since bats seldom bite humans, they represent but a slight danger in most parts of the Americas. On the other hand, those parts of South America where vampire bats occur form an exception, for these bats bite mammals, including humans, in the regular course of business. With their fine, razor-sharp teeth they are capable of making a relatively painless incision, so that a sleeping mammal may not be awakened and the vampire can lick its blood with impunity. Thus the gaucho camping far out on the pampas does not realize that he has been bitten—until he is stricken with rabies.

"Ordinarily the human or animal victim of rabies passes through a stage of irritability during which, in some cases, he may even 'run mad' and attempt to bite every living thing in his path. The course of the illness invariably ends in death. The rabies transmitted by vampire bats, however, has the peculiarity that it takes only a paralytic form: The victim does not show irritability, much less rage, but merely succumbs to spreading paralysis and sinks quietly into death.

"All of the foregoing is well-known scientific fact. Remarkably, however, the Chabaraní told us that the victim of vampire-borne rabies does not always die, but often survives the illness. We did not at first credit their asseverations to this effect. We never took at face value any information provided by the natives without first testing it through observation or experiment in order to separate the kernels of truth from the mass of superstition. In this instance, however, the statements of the Chabaraní were borne out by our own observations: We found that of persons contracting rabies from the bite of a vampire bat, only some seventy percent died of the disease; approximately thirty percent survived.

"We were able to confirm that the rabies virus carried by vampire bats belonged to an aberrant strain, which we called Strain V, distinctly different from the virus of ordinary rabies. Of course, our investigations were hampered by a lack of proper laboratory equipment. Apart from the very little that we had been able to carry with us, we had to work with what we could improvise upon the spot, and only the exceptional ingenuity of Sandoval provided us with means to study the virus at all."

"Sandoval?" asked the professor, with an inquiring glance.

"Ignacio Sandoval, my companion."

Professor Mortimer sat up straight and his eyes widened.

"Ignacio Sandoval! I met him once or twice, many years ago, at international scientific conferences. He was young but extraordinarily gifted and had already so distinguished himself with his remarkable studies in chiropterology that we all believed he was destined to a career of unexampled brilliance. And then... nothing more was heard from him. No one seemed to know what had happened to him. He was with you, then, among these Charabani people?"

"Chabaraní. Yes, Ignacio Sandoval was with me, professor. And I must confess that our discoveries owed more to him than they did to me.

"To continue: Like the normal form of the rabies virus, Strain V attacked the brain. As I've said, only about seventy percent of persons infected with Strain V died of the disease, but we found that in another twenty percent of cases, damage to the cerebral cortex was so severe that the victim's capacity for rational thought was almost completely annihilated and he became forever a moron, hardly distinguishable from a person who had been mentally retarded from birth. This, incidentally, explained our observation that persons of subnormal intelligence were surprisingly frequent among the Chabaraní.

"The remaining ten percent of persons infected with Strain V experienced a recovery that, superficially, appeared complete. Further investigation, however, showed that they too suffered certain aftereffects.

"Before leaving Buenos Aires we had made ourselves thoroughly familiar with all available information concerning Holmberg's ill-fated expedition of 1921. Now, in an effort to learn what had happened to him, we asked all natives whom we encountered whether they had ever heard any stories about Holmberg that might have been handed down by their elders.

"One morning a young fellow whom we had not seen before showed up in the village where we were staying at the time. He was covered from head to toe with ghastly tattoos, he had the bone of a human finger thrust through his nose, and his teeth were filed to points, but for a Chabaraní he was a handsome fellow, to all appearances not more than thirty years old at the outside. We asked him the usual questions, and he replied that he himself had seen Holmberg. Obviously he was lying, since he must have been born several decades after Holmberg's visit. So we challenged him to prove that he was telling the truth by describing Holmberg's appearance. He responded with a description, accurate to the last detail, of Holmberg, of each of his three assistants, and of all of their equipment. It seemed inexplicable. And we subsequently encountered four more natives—none in appearance older than thirty-five years—who likewise claimed to have seen Holmberg and were able to give accurate descriptions of him.

"It took us years to unravel the mystery, but unravel it we did. Given our lack of proper laboratory equipment, the biochemical processes involved necessarily remained in many respects obscure, but in general terms what we found was this:

"The Strain V virus infects not only the nervous system but every cell in the human body. In each cell, the virus attaches itself to the chromosomes in such a way that it permanently halts the aging process. Thus, he who becomes infected with Strain V, and survives, will never grow old, but may live forever. The seemingly young Charabaní who claimed to have seen Holmberg had actually done so, but were older than they looked by several decades at least. Having survived infection with Strain

V, they had become immune to old age."

Osigul paused for a full minute before he continued:

"Professor, imagine a man who would intentionally allow himself to be bitten by an infected vampire bat. He would have nine chances in ten of either dying or becoming a moron, and only one chance in ten of surviving with his faculties intact."

Placing his hands on the professor's desk, Osigul leaned over it, his eyes burning with fanatical passion.

"But he who would take such a desperate gamble—and win it—would become immortal! Think of it, professor! Immortality! The most sought-after prize throughout the ages! The object of more desire and more yearning than the philosopher's stone, which turns lead into gold! More than the perpetual-motion machine, the inexhaustible source of energy! More than the panacea, which cures all diseases—with the exception only of old age!"

Osigul straightened up and continued in a more sober tone.

"We found, however, that there was a catch. When a person has survived the acute stage of infection with Strain V, the infection nevertheless persists in low-grade, chronic form. Fortunately, there is a factor in normal human blood—we called it the C factor—that limits the activity of the virus so that the patient can live without suffering perceptible harm as long as the C factor is present. Less fortunately, the virus gradually impairs the body's capacity to secrete the C factor. Thus, after living with the chronic infection for three or four years, the patient is no longer able to produce the C factor in sufficient quantity, and the virus begins slowly to kill him. His life may drag on painfully for a few years, but in the end he will die... *unless* he can replenish his supply of the C factor from some source outside his own body. What this means in practice, professor, is that, in order to preserve his immortality, the patient must from time to time acquire a fresh quantity of the C factor by drinking the blood of a living human being."

Professor Mortimer had been listening spellbound to his former student, his jaw slack, his mouth open, and his eyes glazed. Now suddenly he seemed to come to himself. He stood up abruptly and snapped.

"Look here, Osigul! Do you actually expect me to believe all this preposterous rubbish!?"

Osigul smiled wanly.

"No professor, I don't expect you to believe it."

He paused briefly, gazing at Professor Mortimer with something like wistful compassion. Then he barked in a peremptory tone:

"¡Ignacio! ¡Cumple con tu deber!"

Instantly Ignacio pounced on the professor, pressing over his nose and mouth a handkerchief saturated with some strong-smelling substance. The professor struggled feebly, but only for a moment, for he swiftly sank into unconsciousness.

***

When Professor Mortimer awoke, the sun had already set. He found himself slumped in his chair and his papers strewn in disorder over his desk.

"Strange!" he said to himself. "I've *never* fallen asleep in my office before. And I've had the oddest dream, too!"

He stood up, and in doing so noticed that he felt extraordinarily weak, as if he had recently lost a great deal of blood. He put his papers in order, took his coat from the hook, stepped out of the office, and locked the door. Luckily he did not live far from the zoology building, so he felt he would be able to reach home safely in spite of his weakness. He crossed the hall, picked his way carefully down the stairs, and left the building through the main door. As he approached the street his path was crossed by a group of high-spirited children wearing costumes. He had forgotten that it was Halloween. A child dressed as a vampire called out, "Trick or treat!" Professor Mortimer fished a quarter from his pocket and held it out toward the boy.

"Here, son," he said.

"I'm Dracula! I want a pint of blood!"

The professor muttered to himself, "Cheeky kid!" and tossed the coin in the boy's direction. Then pensively he turned his steps homeward.

LIST OF WORKS CITED

Alinsky, Saul D., *Rules for Radicals: A Pragmatic Primer for Realistic Radicals*, Vintage Books, Random House, New York, 1989.

Bright, Verne, "The Folklore and History of the Oregon Fever," *Oregon Historical Quarterly*, Vol. 52, Dec. 1951, pp. 241ff.

Bury, J.B., *The Idea of Progress: An Inquiry into its Origin and Growth*, Dover Publications, New York, 1955.

Camp, L. Sprague de, *The Ancient Engineers*, Ballantine Books, New York, 1974.

Carrillo, Santiago, *Eurocomunismo y Estado*, Editorial Crítica, Grupo Editorial Grijalbo, Barcelona, 1977.

Christman, Henry M. (ed.), *Essential Works of Lenin*, Bantam Books, New York, 1966.

Darrach, Brad, "Meet Shaky, the first electronic person," *Life*, Nov. 20, 1970.

De Camp. See Camp, L. Sprague de.

Dick, Everett, *The Dixie Frontier: A Social History*, University of Oklahoma Press, Norman, Oklahoma, 1993.

Durant, Will, *The Story of Civilization*, Part 1, *Our Oriental Heritage*, Book Club Edition, Simon & Schuster, New York, 1954.

Ferris, Warren Angus, *Life in the Rocky Mountains*, edited by Paul C. Phillips, published by F.A. Rosenstock, Old West Publishing Co., Denver, 1940.

Gibbs, W. Wayt, "Seeking the Criminal Element," *Scientific American*, March 1995.

Graham, Hugh Davis, and Ted Robert Gurr (eds.), *Violence in America: Historical and Comparative Perspectives*, Bantam Books, New York, 1970.

Guevara, Che, *On Guerrilla Warfare*, Frederick A. Prager, Inc., Publisher, New York, second printing, 1962.

Hoffer, Eric, *The True Believer*, Harper Perennial, Harper Collins, New York, 1989.

Kaczynski, Theodore John, *Anti-Tech Revolution: Why and How*, Second Edition, Fitch & Madison Publishers, Scottsdale, Arizona, 2020.

Kaczynski, Theodore John, *Technological Slavery*, Fourth Edition, Volume One, Fitch & Madison Publishers, Scottsdale, Arizona, 2022.

Kaczynski, Theodore John, *Technological Slavery*, Second Edition, Feral House, Port Townsend, Washington, 2010.

Lenin. See Christman.

Maas, Peter, *King of the Gypsies*, Viking Press, New York, 1975.

Morris, Desmond, *The Human Zoo*, Kodansha America, Inc., New York, 1996.

Ross, Andrew C., *David Livingstone: Mission and Empire*, Hambledon Continuum, London, 2006.

Rothfels, Hans, *Deutsche Opposition gegen Hitler: Eine Würdigung*, Neue, erweiterte Ausgabe, Fischer Taschenbuch Verlag, Frankfurt am Main, 1986.

Schlissel, Lillian, *Women's Diaries of the Westward Journey*, Schocken Books, New York, 1992.

Selznick, Philip, *The Organizational Weapon: A Study of Bolshevik Strategy and Tactics*, The Free Press of Glencoe, Illinois, 1960.

Shakespeare, William, *As You Like It*.

Tan, Chester C., *Chinese Political Thought in the Twentieth Century*, Doubleday & Company, Garden City, New York, 1971.

Trend, J.B., *Bolívar and the Independence of Spanish America*, published in 1951 under the auspices of the Junta de Gobierno of the United States of Venezuela and under an arrangement made with the University Press of England and the Macmillan Company, New York.

Turnbull, Colin M., *Wayward Servants: The Two Worlds of the African Pygmies*, Natural History Press, Garden City, New York, 1965.

Ulam, Adam B., *Stalin: The Man and His Era*, Beacon Press, Boston, 1987.

Wilson, Timothy D., David A. Reinhard, et al., "Just think: The challenges of the disengaged mind," *Science*, Vol. 345, No. 6192, July 2014, pp. 75–77.

WORKS WITHOUT NAMED AUTHOR

NEB = *The New Encyclopaedia Britannica*, Fifteenth Edition

The Fifteenth Edition has been modified every few years. We put a date in parentheses after NEB—e.g., NEB (2003)—to indicate the copyright date of the particular version of NEB that we cite.

Organizer's Manual, The, Bantam Books, New York, second printing, 1971

Made in the USA
Columbia, SC
11 December 2024